CHILD PROTECTION FOR TEACHERS AND SCHOOLS

A Guide to Good Practice

BEN WHITNEY

KOGAN PAGE

Kogan Page Books for Teachers Series

Career Development for Teachers, Jim Donnelly
Child Protection for Teachers and Schools, Ben Whitney
The Children Act and Schools, Ben Whitney
Education for Citizenship, edited by Eileen Baglin Jones and Neville Jones
A Guide to Creative Tutoring, Stephen Adams
A Handbook for Deputy Heads in Schools, Jim Donnelly
Learning to Behave, edited by Neville Jones and Eileen Baglin Jones
Making Science Education Relevant, Douglas P Newton
Mentoring in Schools, edited by Margaret Wilkin
Middle Managers in Schools and Colleges, Jim Donnelly
Modern Languages for All, Maggie Bovair and Keith Bovair
Parental Choice in Education, edited by Mark Halstead
Themes and Dimensions of the National Curriculum, edited by Geoffrey Hall
The Truth About Truancy, Ben Whitney

First published in 1996

Kogan Page Limited
120 Pentonville Road
London N1 9JN

© Ben Whitney, 1996

British Library Cataloguing in Publication Data

A CIP record for this book is available from the British Library.

ISBN 0 7494 1834 6

Typeset by Kogan Page
Printed and bound in Great Britain by Biddles Ltd, Guildford and King's Lynn

Contents

Preface

While writing this book, I have had the opportunity to organize and deliver child protection training for designated school staff, governors and inter-professional groups. While the book inevitably reflects the procedures I know best, I hope this also shows that it is rooted in real situations and it has been greatly revised in the light of the experience I have picked up on the way. I am grateful to all my colleagues, especially those from the Mid-Staffordshire Trainers' Group for their collective wisdom, which I have borrowed at every available opportunity! The text includes references to the most recent DfEE circulars, issued in late 1995. The views expressed are my own responsibility and do not necessarily reflect the policy of Staffordshire ACPC or its member agencies.

Ben Whitney
February 1996

Introduction

Child abuse

- What exactly is child abuse?
- Who should I tell if a child in my class has an injury?
- What do social workers do when I make a referral?
- What happens at a case conference?
- Am I allowed to touch children?
- Where can I find help?
- What if a child makes an allegation against me?

Many teachers are worried about child abuse; not least because they fear they could become the subject of an investigation themselves in circumstances that might end their careers. There has been a significant increase in the last few years in the number of allegations made against teachers by children. Parents often take the child's 'side' in such disputes and reputations can be ruined forever. Some incidents in which teachers have used what they see as reasonable restraint against children in class have become major news stories or ended up in the courts. Professionals outside education can sometimes seem unsympathetic and over-zealous; the media are always ready to blow things out of all proportion.

While the significance of genuine causes for concern must never be minimized (and they do happen), the majority of such cases have uncovered little evidence of a serious problem, although often not until months of suspension, uncertainty and stress have passed. Some accused teachers have never recovered from the ordeal; a few have never worked again. In this sense, child abuse, and the law designed to detect, deal with and prevent it, have become something of a problem within education.

Many feel that it is the teachers who need protecting – not only from children intent on malicious trouble making, but from those (or their parents) who are capable of using intimidation, verbal abuse and violence, even within the classroom. The unions have talked of 10-year-old 'thugs' who have no place in mainstream schools. There have been a few examples of dreadful injuries. Some teachers have become anxious about touching children, even out of friendship or to give reassurance, for fear that an innocent gesture might be misunderstood or used against them later.

Some of these worries are well founded. There are children with emotional and behavioural difficulties (a rather more professional term than 'thug'), who may require special educational provision and whose needs have never been properly assessed or met. Failure to address such issues is bound to lead to frustration and an increased risk of violence on all sides. The laudable emphasis on listening to children and giving them a voice, which has become more commonplace since the Children Act 1989, has been misinterpreted by some as requiring us all to give children whatever they want and to accept without question anything they say.

A few agencies and individuals seem to have elevated the status of children above all sensible levels, giving them a total veto over anything they do not wish to do, forgetting, for example, that it is the *welfare* of children which is paramount in the Children Act, not their *wishes*. I have heard statements such as 'children always tell the truth' or claims that no child would ever deliberately make up an allegation against a teacher without some genuine basis to their story.

On the other hand, teachers can be equally naive: a school once assured me they had taken all reasonable precautions against possible abuse on a school trip abroad by making sure that the male teacher only checked the boys' dormitory! Men, in particular do need to be careful if they choose to work with young children or volunteer for extra duties after school hours. Some seem rather too unaware of the issues and of the need to use their common sense to avoid suspicion. A few seem to have forgotten that we are dealing with children, not the Mafia! The whole area has become fraught with anxieties and, in the face of so many other things to do, teachers could be forgiven for thinking that perhaps the tasks arising from abused and abusing children are best left to others.

There is undoubtedly a real defensiveness among professionals and genuine difficulties in relationships between teachers, children, parents and, particularly, social workers. This is most unfortunate. It was the intention of the Children Act that we would all work more closely together, not be driven further apart. There is a feeling among many teachers that the Act is a threat or an excuse for anarchy, when it should be the focus of our combined efforts to 'safeguard and promote the welfare of children'. This reaction has obscured the vision of what is most important: the *vital* role of school staff within the network of caring agencies for preventing, detecting and responding to child abuse.

THE AIMS OF THIS BOOK

Child protection

More child protection referrals come from schools than from any other source. My aim is to increase competence in dealing with that awesome responsibility. It is important to recognize the very real worries with which I began and not just deal with the requirements of law and good practice as if each of us comes to such issues without prior feelings.

However, teachers sometimes forget that *all* of us who work with children run the same risks. These include greater threats to our physical safety when visiting families in their own homes and the risks attached to being alone with children, trying to persuade them to return to school, driving them to appointments, taking them on trips, or making them do things against their will. Later in the book I hope to offer a sensible and realistic framework within which teachers can operate and play a small part in easing the anxieties while remaining properly vigilant.

We must keep a sense of proportion: social workers should not see an abuser in every classroom or behind every allegation, however unsubstantiated. Teachers must not allow themselves to be distracted from their crucial role in recognizing and referring abuse because of an over-emphasis on their own vulnerability. The issue of personal risk is important, but it must not dominate. The Children Act is an excellent piece of legislation – not some charter for trendy do-gooders and out-of-control children. We must know how to use it for everyone's mutual benefit.

Few teachers know the Act as well as they should, but its framework of law and practice is an essential part of our responsibility for pastoral care. It does not lay down anything like the restrictions on adults that some believe, nor give children carte blanche as they sometimes claim. Knowing what it says, and being confident of the teacher's role in interagency procedures, provides not only full protection for children but increased security for the teacher. Fulfilling this primary task properly makes it more likely that false allegations will be avoided. Caring teachers should have nothing to fear from the legislation.

This book brings together a number of themes under the general heading of 'child protection'. Traditionally some of these fall together; others are sometimes overlooked or dealt with in different contexts. The emphasis is on child *protection* not on child *abuse*. Perhaps 'child abuse courses' for teachers have given the wrong impression! I am primarily interested in positive strategies for prevention, detection and response rather than aiming to give a detailed account of the various forms of abuse and their consequences. This is not a specialist handbook for those whose professional role involves direct work with abused and at-risk children or adult survivors. It is intended for all teachers and anyone else, especially governors, non-teaching staff and education welfare officers, who wishes to be alert to these wider issues.

Summary

Chapter 1 gives a brief contextual and historical introduction, drawing attention to the rediscovery of child abuse since the 1970s and to some of the findings from inquiry reports into major incidents from Maria Colwell (DHSS, 1974) to the Cleveland Report (Butler-Sloss 1988) which have brought us to where we are today. What lessons have been learned which have led to the approach to child protection in the 1990s?

Chapter 2 gives an overview of current definitions and understandings of abuse, together with a summary of both law and practice. The focus is on the Children Act 1989 and the government guidance that stems from it. The statutory tasks of the Area Child Protection Committee (ACPC) and its procedures are outlined in some detail as teachers are often not fully aware of them.

Chapter 3 is the core of the book and develops the concept of the 'child-protecting school' by looking at a range of issues which need to be addressed by any school seeking to meet the requirements of the Department of Health (DoH), the Department for Education and Employment (DfEE) and the Office for Standards in Education (OF-STED). It includes a step-by-step guide to the role of the teacher in the child protection process and also examines the issue of bullying, often overlooked in this context. Children need to feel safe at school, not just safe to disclose what is happening outside. Bullies have needs too, and may also be children at risk.

Chapter 4 deals with the part-time employment of children: again this is not usually seen as a child protection issue but is being viewed increasingly as such alongside other possibly abusive situations. While the Department of Health carries lead responsibility in this area (from within its child protection section), LEAs are responsible at local level and teachers have a key role to play. An European Council (EC) Directive in 1994 has given this issue a higher profile.

Chapter 5 considers the question of allegations against teachers and other staff. It includes an analysis of the issues arising from a report into abuse at an LEA nursery school, discussion of new procedures for protecting teachers from unsubstantiated allegations, DfEE circulars, and guidance from the Council of Local Education Authorities and teacher organizations.

Appendix 1 offers a model policy for child protection now that all schools are expected to have one. Appendix 2 includes a selection of ideas that could be used by a Professional Development Coordinator or designated teacher in planning training for colleagues in child protection, together with some resources for addressing child protection and child employment issues in the classroom.

Appendix 3 contains an extensive glossary giving over 100 definitions of many of the words and phrases commonly used by other professionals which may not be immediately familiar to all teachers attending case conferences, etc. It may be helpful to refer to it throughout the book whenever a specialist term is encountered as they are not normally defined within the text itself.

1

From Poor Law to Protection

AN HISTORICAL PERSPECTIVE

Attitudes and values

Child protection, although not child abuse, has a relatively brief history. Children had a pretty rough time in British society, especially those from poor and minority groups, at least until the later years of the 19th century. The idea that other people might in some way be responsible for what goes on within family life has never received universal acceptance. The history of the legislation shows a constant swinging of the pendulum between interventionist and more *laissez-faire* approaches, nowhere more so than in the last 20 years when there have been, in turn, scandals about failure to act in time and complaints of excessive or unnecessary intervention.

We are far from clear about the boundaries of 'reasonable chastisement' by parents (a legal defence against prosecution), and the value of protection systems (ie, what exactly do we want as a society in this area?). Smacking is not illegal within the home and is actively advocated by some, including a number of religious groups, as an essential means of disciplining children. A major review of research published in 1995 quotes a study by the Thomas Coram Research Unit which found that 75 per cent of babies under one year old are hit by their parent and 91 per cent of children as a whole are hit at some time (DoH, 1995). Moreover, there is a strong sense of privacy in our society. Evidence of this is the assumption that parenting is intuitive and best left to the discretion and judgement of the individuals concerned, with little or no outside intervention, rather than it being a suitable subject for formal education.

The debate about the merits of physical punishment while children are cared for outside the family shows no sign of ending. There is obvious ambivalence within the Department of Health with constant changes to the guidance, even though the boundaries for teachers are much more clearcut than those, for example, for childminders. Some prominent politicians and educational professionals make no secret of the fact that they would like to return to a time when teachers could assert their authority through the cane or the slipper (still legal, though rare, within the independent sector).

We live in a culture which emphasizes toughness and sees violence as a means to resolving conflict: harsher regimes for offending children are popular and many feel that care settings are too 'soft'. To what extent should reasonable restraint be used against an aggressive child? Few people really know or care. Many did not see what the fuss was about when 'pindown' was used to contain children; nor do they want to know what goes on behind the doors of residential establishments.

Interagency feelings

Equally, a few, highly publicized cases, in which social workers have appeared to act without justification or have appeared not to act when they should have done so, have caused something of a crisis in interagency perceptions. I have heard school governors and teachers say that they would never pass information about a child to the social services for fear that something dreadful and unstoppable would result. Professionals sometimes caricature and stereotype each other: when under pressure, there is often a temptation to retreat into blame, denial and self-protection.

Teachers and social workers can deliberately misunderstand each other. Social workers are irritated by the fact that most school staff are not available for 12 weeks in a year or sometimes have unrealistic expectations of what can be achieved by troubled children. Teachers often see social workers as less than objective; too much allied with the particular child and thus generally unaware of the needs of all the other children in the school and the adults who work with them. Some medical professionals, in particular seem to have a very low opinion of others with whom they are supposed to work. There are constant claims of colleagues not sharing what is going on or not respecting each other's experience.

But we have a duty to work together and to forge new partnerships both with one another and with parents and children. Out of what are now recognized as past disasters, there is supposed to be a new consensus based on a shared commitment to the welfare of children in need. The child's well-being is intended to be our common focus. For teachers, whose primary responsibility is not in the field of child protection, it may be helpful to begin by charting some of the key issues of the recent past, in order to understand how we have come to where we are.

Children in history

Acknowledgement of children as individuals in their own right, and therefore with rights to dignity and respect, is a very new phenomenon. It could be argued that we have yet to accept it to any significant extent. The UN Convention on the Rights of the Child (1989) had to spell it out because it cannot be assumed. The contrasting idea, that children are primarily extensions of their parents, part of their 'goods and chattels', has a rather longer history. Children have traditionally been seen as disposable assets – much the same as property. Until the Children Act 1989, roughly the same philosophy operated in dealing with children following the divorce of their parents.

In any society beset with high infant mortality, the sense of a child's distinct personality and identity is inevitably lost. I remember seeing a gravestone in an ancient churchyard: 'Sacred to the memory of Florence... who had several (unnamed) children, most of whom died at birth'. It has been compulsory to register births for only a century or so (since 1874), in the aftermath of the Infant Life Protection Act 1872. Many children before then must have lived and died with scarcely anyone outside the family being aware of the fact.

In P Aries' book *Centuries of Childhood* (1973, but now out of print), the author describes the 'benign indifference' of parents towards their children in medieval times in the sense that they should be treated with kindness but with no real emotional attachment to their best interests. Aries acknowledges that others have seen the relationship as rather less than benign, with parents rapidly losing interest after the social significance of the birth had passed. Many abandoned the care and upbringing of their children to others, taking little or no part in their life from then on.

In the past, children moved rapidly into the adult world, with little or no developmental stages between infancy and adulthood. They soon achieved the status of workers in poorer families; while for the more wealthy, children might be treated as ornaments, marriageable bargaining-counters or as masters-in-waiting. By the 17th century contemporary writers were complaining that parents had become over indulgent. Theological understandings of children as 'unspoilt', and consequently closer to God than adults, fostered a climate of sentimentality in which children came to be seen as precious, but fragile; at risk from darker forces and therefore, to be kept apart and, in one sense, protected.

The innocence of childhood was also a strong theme in the 18th century, in, for example, the poetry of Blake and Wordsworth. This verse is from a poem in the *Songs of Innocence* written by William Blake in celebration of the annual service for charity school children at St Paul's Cathedral:

> *O what a multitide they seem'd, these flowers of London town;*
> *Seated in companies they sit with radiance all their own.*
> *The hum of the multitudes was there, but multitudes of lambs,*
> *Thousands of little boys and girls raising their innocent hands.*

Yet, at the same time, in an increasingly urban society, the exploitation of children at work moved from being a rural, family-oriented phenomenon into an organized economic consequence of increased industrialization. This led to the wholesale abuse of poor children for profit, including child prostitution on a scale which would certainly be considered unacceptable today. More middle-class children, however, retained their place as objects of innocence, and yet in need of moral restraint and discipline, contrasting images perhaps more prevalent in Victorian Britain than ever before. Each Christmas, millions of parents and children still sing:

> *And through all his wondrous childhood*
> *He would honour and obey,*
> *Love and watch the lowly mother*
> *In whose gentle arms he lay:*
> *Christian children all must be*
> *Mild, obedient, good as he.*   (Mrs C F Alexander 1818–95)

Current trends

My reading of the 20th century is as a series of similarly conflicting images of childhood. The range of statutory and protective arrangements has never been greater, but how do we actually feel about children? Changing social trends in marriage and family life have primarily been driven by adults, with children's needs not the prime concern. Bringing up children has generally been relegated to a second-class activity, less important than economic productivity and frequently penalized by the tax and employment system. Increasing numbers of women (one in five of the relevant age range) are choosing to have no children at all, some at least on the grounds that they represent an unwanted tie and a financial burden.

We have largely assumed that with the greater opportunities open to children for education and independent choice, they will be able to manage the emotional adjustments which are now required of them in order to cope with less stable parental relationships and the decline of the extended family. (Three out of four children experience some change in their parental relationships before the age of 16.) Children seem to want to get the business of childhood over with as quickly as possible; more than ever we are being encouraged to see them as little adults with their own views and perspectives and their need for space to be themselves.

However, I also detect a growing sense of such liberated children as a threat resulting in a desire for greater control over them. We may not expect them just to be seen and not heard, but they are still supposed to do as they are told, not least within the education system. Few schools recognize the concept of 'children's rights'. Many parents seem to feel that controlling children is essentially the school's task and expect staff to teach children proper behaviour on their behalf. There would be no shortage of parents willing to allow teachers to use physical punishment. Many teachers could tell stories of the parent presenting their 5-year-old at school, already out of control and expecting the school to do something about it!

Politicians can make much capital out of any initiative designed to remove more troublesome children from circulation – from truancy patrols to secure training centres and even military 'glasshouses'. The spectre of children rampaging through shopping centres when they should be at school was deliberately raised by an education minister in the early 1990s, despite the total lack of evidence that such things actually happen. It is too early to say just yet, but I suspect that the Jamie Bulger case of 1993 will prove to be a lasting icon of our time, with the tabloid photographs of the two 10-year olds acquiring the hate status which used to be reserved for adult killers. Some would actually have wanted to see them hang. The fact that they were children somehow made them to be feared *more*, not less, as any rational consideration might suggest.

Few people would see this as a tragedy involving *three* lost child-hoods. Little or no concession was made in the public's mind for the fact that they were so young; yet at other times children are seen as having a right to be understood as vulnerable individuals in an adult world, whose 'welfare' should be paramount. Poor children are often stigmatized along with their parents; cuts in welfare benefits to single mothers, for example, impact on the children just as much as on the parent. Yet we also talk of children as in need of protection and that agencies have a duty to look after them. It is no wonder that teachers are sometimes confused over what exactly society wants them to do with children and young people in their care; society does not seem to have a clear idea either.

Public policy

The history of public policy to protect and safeguard the interests of children goes back at least to the original Poor Law legislation of the 17th century. The Act of 1601 was perhaps the first recognition that some families needed intervention from outside in order to ensure a child's right to basic survival. However, this Act, like the Poor Law Reform Act 230 years later, was essentially punitive rather than protective. Failing parents were seen as weak and their children in need of rescue so that, in the care of the state, they might learn to work hard and overcome the inadequacies which had led their family into difficulty in the first place.

A series of 19th-century laws created offences relating to direct physical cruelty towards children. The threshold, however, tended to be quite high. In a celebrated case in 1847 (R v Renshaw), a 10-day old baby had been left by its mother in a ditch, wrapped in a large piece of flannel. The baby was found quite soon, evidently unharmed by the experience. The mother was acquitted of attempted murder but then also acquitted of even a common assault, as no actual 'injury or inconvenience' could be proven.

The Poor Law Amendment Act of 1868 made it an offence for a parent wilfully to neglect a child's needs for food, clothing, medical aid and housing in such a way as harmed, or was likely to harm their health. Criminal legislation, to be enforced against the parent, was the primary concern, rather than focussing on the needs of the child. Some commentators apparently thought that the intervention, which usually deprived the child of their parent and left them to be brought up as a pauper in wholly unsatisfactory institutions, probably did the child more harm than good!

NSPCC created

The earliest concerted attempt to address issues of what we would now call 'child abuse', followed the creation of the British Society Against Cruelty to Children in Liverpool in 1883. Many local societies of this kind merged to form the National Society for the Prevention of Cruelty to Children (NSPCC) in 1890, which, by the turn of the century had set up a national network of inspectors. Much of the work was commendably preventative in a way which often seems less true of the recent past: working with parents to keep families together rather than protecting children by removing them from home, and so relieving their parents of their proper responsibilities.

The Prevention of Cruelty to and Protection of Children Act of 1889 was undoubtedly a milestone. This not only made the ill-treatment and neglect of children an offence, it also made more thorough provision for the subsequent care of the child by a 'fit person'. The Poor Law (Children) Act of the same year gave authority for the Guardians to take over the parental rights of a child already in their care if they were satisfied that the parents should not do so. The Prevention of Cruelty to Children Act 1904 first gave the local authorities powers to remove children from their parents, including those who had not actually been convicted of a criminal offence against them but where it was felt that the child's needs required it.

Since then there has been a continuous debate about the relative rights of parents and the appropriate powers of the state. The Children and Young Persons Act 1933, still in force in part, and which first used the concept of 'the welfare of the child', erred on the side of intervention and removal. The Children Act 1948 emphasized more preventative services and gave local authorities a duty to rehabilitate children within their family of origin wherever possible. The Children and Young Person's Act 1969 tended to increase the priority given to caring for children away from home, though this may not necessarily have been its intention. The Children Act 1989 is perhaps more in tune with the approach of the 1948 Act, though there has been growing concern that too much emphasis is still being placed on investigation and not enough on prevention and family support (DoH, 1995 op cit).

Child abuse rediscovered

Many writers put 'rediscovered' in inverted commas at this point as it never really went away. Parents went on being convicted of cruelty and neglect. Incest and abandonment were always on the statute books, though again, the emphasis tended to be on the crime rather than on the needs of the child. Freud had reported that some of his patients claimed they had been sexually abused as children, though he later suggested, as some still do, that such accounts might owe more to hysteria than reality. But even as late as the early 1970s, there was little emphasis on child protection; there were few local systems of registration and an Open University textbook on child abuse (Carver, 1978) gave just six lines to sexual abuse.

In 1946 John Caffey, a specialist in paediatric radiology in the United States, first noticed that some injuries to the long bones of infants had been caused by trauma/injury rather than by disease. He did not, however, speculate as to their cause. Silverman, in 1953 attributed such injuries to parental carelessness; Woolley and Evans in 1955 attributed them to deliberate acts by the babies' parents/carers. The growth in techniques of radiology, and the extreme young age of the children involved, gave the issue a new and more public profile.

It was not until 1962 that Dr Henry Kempe, in a speech at the University of Colorado, coined the term 'battered child syndrome'. He reported research by colleagues all over the USA resulting in a network of registration and protection of children at risk, or who had been injured, being set up by 1967. Kempe's terminology was taken up in Britain almost immediately. In 1963 Griffiths and Moynihan – two orthopaedic surgeons – and Cameron et al in 1966 published papers on the issue and a memorandum was circulated to all doctors.

However, by 1978 the Open University text referred to above, was suggesting that 'battered baby' may be too limited a concept, and that 'non-accidental injury' or 'child abuse' was more appropriate. Too much emphasis on the image of helpless babies, and on actual acts of physical violence, was obscuring the more general question of children who were failing to thrive or at risk in other ways. Although the first 'at-risk' registers were set up in Britain in the early 1970s, it was not until there was a series of public enquiries that the issue became a real priority. British social policy tends to be highly influenced by individual cases, and it is to those stories over the last 20 years that we now turn.

LEARNING FROM OUR MISTAKES

Conceptualizing abuse

In their extremely interesting book (Reder et al, 1993), Peter Reder, Sylvia Duncan and Moira Gray chart the history of a series of public inquiries into child abuse tragedies between 1973 and 1989. As the title *Beyond Blame* makes clear, the purpose of their analysis, and mine in drawing upon it, is to go beyond the expression of moral outrage and the allocation of blame, either to parents, professionals or 'the system' and to see what may be learnt from the experience.

They chart a sequence of stages through which the concept of 'child abuse' must go in order to appreciate its full significance. The social construction of child abuse is rather like a spring; an evolving spiral of legislation, attitudes and inquiries which moves forward through time and in which three elements interact:

- social values about children and families;
- professional practice;
- theories and knowledge.

As society progressively alters its attitudes to children and their welfare, expectations of parents are reviewed and refined. Unacceptable standards of care are defined, which warrant state intervention. Professional practice is itself sensitive to prevailing social beliefs and is guided by contemporary theories and knowledge, while new research is prompted by questions arising from professional work and social beliefs. From time to time, social attitudes become consolidated through political initiatives and legislation. At other times, social concern about state interventions leads to public inquiries, the results of which help to modify practice and may lay the groundwork for new legislation.

(Reder et al, 1993, p 6)

A five-stage model

Child protection evolves; it is not a static concept. Kempe and Kempe (1978) have identified a five-stage process of professional recognition of the issues:

- a denial that physical or sexual abuse exists to any extent and that which is acknowledged is attributed to 'maniacs/monsters', etc;
- the community pays attention to the more lurid forms of abuse or the 'battered child'. More effective ways of dealing with severe physical abuse are found, together with strategies for prevention;
- abuse is handled better; wider concepts such as failing to thrive and neglect are included. More subtle forms of abuse are recognized;
- society recognizes emotional abuse, scapegoating and patterns of severe rejection;
- attention is paid to the existence and needs of children who are being sexually abused, and those adults with a past history of being abused as children.

New questions

It is not that we have now reached stage 5 and so all is well just because sexual abuse is high up the child protection agenda. We are all at different places, and at different places at different times. The tabloid press has never got beyond stage 1! There has been a long-running debate going on among child care professionals about the concept of 'neglect' and whether too many children's needs of this kind are being ignored. Many teachers would identify with this issue: the long-term dysfunctional families where children do not thrive but do not actually get hurt and who often do not seem to get the protection they need.

Some are questioning the very existence of any kind of ritual or organized element which others have argued is at the heart of much sexual and some physical abuse; yet others are asking if we are right to confine our definition of 'abuse' to what goes on within the family and, if so, whether children who witness violence between their parents should be included. Should racism, poverty and poor housing be seen as abuse; do unborn children have a right to protection?

Headteachers have occasionally told me that they do not have any children in their school who might ever be at risk. This is because they have in mind a particular image of the abused child or the abusing family which is limiting their perceptions. Other professionals, however, stress that abuse knows no barriers of class, race, culture, religion or community and claim that we only ever know about the tip of the iceberg in middle-class families who do not have contact with agencies for other reasons.

The tragedies of recent years can be explained by varying combinations of incompetence, lack of resources, parental inadequacy and professional failure. But the issue is also complicated by the fact that there is no absolute consensus about the boundaries of abuse and involvement by any professional requires an element of judgement and personal evaluation. This is one reason why the job is so difficult.

'How do I know when it's abuse?' is the cry of many a teacher on the training sessions I have led. How *can* we know, until we know what we mean by the word 'abuse'? Is what I mean, the same as you mean? And is what we mean the same as is meant by this family, this community, this religious group, this neighbourhood, this culture, this society? Picking over the legacy of past disasters should help increase our competence, but not necessarily our confidence, as the more we know the more confusing things may become. It is perhaps this uncertainty which leads at least some teachers into denial. This is the first and most important hurdle to be overcome for effective interagency practice.

The cases

Some of the cases reviewed by Reder et al (1993) achieved more notoriety than others. Maria Colwell (DHSS, 1974) gained a particular status as the first such incident for some time, though there had been enquiries into the deaths of Denis O'Neill in 1945 and Graham Bagnall in 1973. The 1970s and 1980s witnessed an explosion of this kind of investigation and response, together with growing public awareness. The cases of O'Neill, Colwell, Jasmine Beckford in 1985 and Kimberley Carlile in 1987 all led directly or indirectly to new legislation.

The authors reviewed 35 cases, all but one of which led to fatalities. There were many other incidents during the review period 1973–89 but not all enquiries were made public. (There are about 80–100 such child deaths a year, though the numbers have been falling.) Not all the reports focussed directly on the child concerned; one of them, Max Piazzani in 1974, does not even mention his age! Some were more concerned with the adults and how the criminal evidence against them had been collected. They varied from 13 pages to 585 and information was sometimes sketchy. There was no common framework within which such investigations took place and no central register of all such reports published.

Public awareness of child protection issues tends to be dominated by the cases that go wrong. This trend has continued into the 1990s. In the 1970s and 1980s, the concern was primarily about under-intervention and vulnerable children who had not been adequately protected, with regular calls for much greater vigilance and action by the authorities. These cases focus on children killed or neglected *by those looking after them* – an emphasis on action by parents/carers is key to which kinds of behaviour normally come within the definition of 'child abuse' (see Chapter 2).

As will be seen later, I argue for a wider definition when it comes to 'child protection' but the (relatively) rare circumstances of children whose trust is betrayed by their families or carers, tends to generate particular interest and recrimination. Teachers need to be consciously aware of their practice in this area; in part as 'carers' themselves (*in loco parentis*), so that any inappropriateness in their own behaviour is identified, and in part as agents of public policy with statutory responsibilities towards other people's children. The conclusions to be drawn from this series of tragedies are therefore particularly significant in setting the context for our practice.

The findings

Reder et al (1993) note that a common strand within the enquiries is the failure of inter-professional communication. When you have a moment, write down all those agencies and individuals who might have some role to play in the protection of children. Anyone who has ever attended a case conference will recognize the problem; there never seem to be enough chairs! The authors' analysis identifies five key elements in this inter-relationship which affected the outcomes of the cases they reviewed.

Professionals need to feel secure in their own work setting in order to undertake the demanding tasks of child protection
It is tempting to say this alone will account for any shortcomings in the education service. Faced with year-on-year budget cuts and the non-replacement of experienced staff, the shrinking of LEA support, the imminence of yet more local government re-organization and the possibility of a change of central government, on top of all the legislative and philosophical changes of the last 10 years, expecting teachers, education welfare officers and others to feel secure in the current climate is wholly unrealistic. Add to this the personal stress involved in such work, the anxieties felt by many teachers which I referred to earlier, together with the general feeling that good practice in child protection is often unrecognized and undermined by other pressures to achieve success in more measurable terms, and it is clear that there is still ample scope for failure.

Professional networks which are 'closed' tend to encourage fixed views about cases and cut people off from important or contrary information which they need to have
Professional systems can become closed for a number of reasons: too much emphasis on our own professional arena; too much association with like-minded individuals who simply reinforce our current perceptions; and stereotyped views of others which lead us to mistrust them or resist losing control to them. These characteristics seem to be very common among both childcare professionals and teachers.

The key is surely in enabling people to train together and to establish personal contacts. Staff turnover alone can make this difficult. However, social workers, health visitors, etc do not usually need their employers to recruit supply cover so that they can be released from day-to-day duties. Teachers often cannot take up the opportunities which are available to other professionals. They tend to want to be trained by and with other teachers and do not always give similar status to those with different expertise. Addressing all of this is crucial for good practice.

*Closed networks lead to polarization so that there is no shared agenda
between agencies. Children and families are given different messages at
different times*

The researchers suggest that this tends to happen unconsciously
rather than deliberately. But the effect is obvious. I would argue that
this is largely caused by the legislative and administrative framework
within which we are all asked to work. Social workers operate the
Children Act from within a social services department. Teachers
deliver the national curriculum and league table statistics under the
(increasingly) arms-length control of the LEA or as entirely independent institutions. Headteachers and governors work to the requirements of OFSTED. Educational psychologists make assessments
of special educational need, Education Welfare Officers (EWOs)
respond to absence, and school nurses monitor children's health, etc.

These are the jobs we are employed to do; we often have little room
for flexibility, especially in the world of performance indicators and
target objectives. Our political masters are in competition for scarce
resources; our employers are setting their own agendas across a wide
range of responsibilities in which child protection is given virtually
total priority within a Social Services Department (SSD), but little
significance within an LEA. There is no child-centred approach as
such; no Ministry/Department for Children to hold it all together. We
are all just employees fulfilling our agencies' requirements which are
often in conflict with each other or, at least, not planned in a coordinated way. No wonder things go wrong.

*Child protection fails when more emphasis is placed on hierarchies of power
than on individuals' knowledge of a particular situation*

Here, in contrast perhaps to previous comments, I would come to the
defence of the teacher. It is clear that for all the talk of interagency
practice, social workers are in charge of child protection. Of course
others have key roles, and courts actually have the greater say in one
sense, but teachers are sometimes the last to find out what is happening, even though children spend 30 hours a week in their care.
Decisions sometimes seem to be made by those who have little direct
involvement with the child without much consultation with those
who know them best.

There is an ambivalence about education in the care setting which
can lead to disempowerment of those who have real knowledge of
children's needs. If, for example, EWOs are sometimes ignored because they are not teachers, there are other times when their insights
are overlooked because they are not seen as proper social workers
either, even when professionally qualified. We need boundaries to

our practice (see below), but all those involved in education also need to feel that their professional expertise is respected, even allowing for their lack of *legal* authority in this context.

Where professionals are confused about their roles, or try to carry out the responsibilities of others, practice breaks down and children are put at unnecessary risk

A teacher who acts like a social worker deprives that child of both roles done properly. We have to know our limits. These are largely defined for us by local procedures. There is no room for enthusiastic amateurs who decide to sort the problem out themselves. This can be very difficult for teachers. They care very much about the children who give cause for concern. They do not necessarily want to hand the child over to some other professional whose actions they cannot control.

'Maybe we'll just contact the parents ourselves and ask them about this allegation the child is making' (thereby alerting them to a potential investigation in advance) or 'Let's get the child to tell us all about it before we do anything else' (thereby leading to accusations of 'coaching' or contamination of the evidence). There can be no absolute guarantee of confidentiality: 'just between the two of us' (we will decide about it for ourselves). The teacher has a *duty* to consult; they must do *their* job, not undo someone else's.

It was the significance of issues like these which led to the rapid increase in priority given to child protection in the 1980s. There is a greater expectation in society that those with the care of other people's children will recognize their duties in this area. Clearly we all still have a great deal to learn and much of this book will involve going over this ground again because we need to be constantly monitoring our practice. Recognizing the insights of this research will at least increase the likelihood that the task will be done more effectively, by teachers and by everyone else. There is, however, another side to the coin.

The Cleveland Inquiry

Public confidence in child protection services took a further battering in the late 1980s; this time, not because of a lack of intervention but due to a perceived excess of it. No one died because of Cleveland, but it came to dominate public thinking. In May and June 1987, sexual abuse was 'diagnosed' in 121 children from 57 families at Middlesborough General Hospital. Most of them were removed from their parents' care by court order. There was widespread concern in both press and parliament about these cases with claims that the degree of actual evidence produced was limited and the methods of diagnosis unreliable. There was a strong sense that the action may have added to the children's problems rather than alleviated them, let alone the issues of natural justice involved. (There were other examples later in Rochdale, Orkney and elsewhere.)

The Cleveland Inquiry did not lead directly to the Children Act 1989. Much of the thinking which paved the way for the Act had already been done elsewhere, particularly in the Review of the Law on Child Care and Family Services in 1987. But the conclusions of the final report fitted more closely the now prevailing philosophy and it may be seen as catching the emerging mood. Cleveland led to an overtly political debate, partly under the influence of a prominent local MP, so it is a key milestone in the formation of both policy and practice.

The actions of educational professionals were not a major focus of the report. But to complete this survey of the rediscovery of child protection, it is useful to identify some of its major conclusions which then became the key philosophical context for professional practice in the 1990s. If there are lessons to be learned from the mistakes of the 1970s and early 1980s, more recent concern has focussed, not only on interagency failures, (which were again an issue here), but also on clarifying the basis on which society should be interfering at all. Perhaps this is the more fundamental question.

Does our intervention achieve what is best for *children*, not simply what is best for the adults who live and work with them or for society? Has it all become too much a question of following procedures and covering our backs rather than delivering an improvement in the quality of children's lives? Current thinking is intended to ensure that the child's welfare is at the centre in a way which has never, perhaps, been attempted so self-consciously before. Whether or not this objective is being achieved is another question (and a different book!), but that is supposed to be the focus.

Recommendations

The Cleveland report made a number of recommendations which have now become axiomatic in child protection.

The child is a person and not an object of concern
This has become a crucial concept in post-Cleveland practice. Children not only need professionals to explain to them what is happening, they are also entitled to participate in the decision-making and to have their wishes and feelings taken into account. They have a right to put those views to a court deciding what should happen to them (though those wishes need not necessarily be followed), and not to be subjected to repeated examinations and interviews. It was this idea

which led to the introduction of prerecorded video interviews for court proceedings and much of this language is repeated in the Children Act and its accompanying guidance. Protection should have the *child's* needs at the centre.

Parents are entitled to be treated with greater respect and kept more fully informed

'Partnership' has become the buzz word of the 1990s here as elsewhere. Decisions should not be made by professionals without the implications of those decisions being discussed with parents at every stage. Parents should not be left isolated and without support and they are entitled to have their rights fully explained, even if they are under investigation. If children are removed into care, parents' rights of contact should be clarified in writing and they should have the opportunity to challenge the decisions in a court. Parents have a right to know about case conferences and to attend unless their presence will seriously act against the child's best interests. *All* professionals, not just social workers, are expected to demonstrate this commitment to openness, now reinforced in the Children Act by the concept of 'parental responsibility' as a permanent status.

Statutory powers should be used only when necessary and last for the minimum time possible

The 'place of safety order' was removed by the Children Act and the general principle established that orders should only be made when they are better for the child than no order. This has led to a significant change in professional practice to working by agreement (though there are now some signs that the number of statutory interventions is rising again). As will be seen in the next chapter, orders are more limited in both time and effect. Orders should not be made without careful thought; there should be no sense that courts will simply 'rubber stamp' decisions made by agencies or that highly interventionist powers will be quickly granted by magistrates in pyjamas!

Careful consideration should be given to the operation of interagency procedures

All agencies must agree a framework for the protection of children and each must accept their appropriate responsibility. While social services and (to a lesser extent) the police, carry prime responsibility, procedures should operate under agreement between *all* those involved. Suspicions should be carefully monitored and assessments made, through consultation with all those with knowledge of the child/family.

Much of this will now seem stunningly obvious to anyone who has had personal experience of child protection work in the last few years.

That is perhaps a measure of how much has changed. The journey through history will no doubt introduce more changes in future, but understanding the past helps us to see how these principles have emerged and how significant they are. All that follows must be understood in the light of them as we now examine the way in which law and practice currently operate, both in defining abuse and responding to it.

REFERENCES

Aries, P (1973) *Centuries of Childhood*, Penguin, London (out of print)

Bainham, A (1993) *Children: The Modern Law*, Jordan Publishing Ltd, Bristol

Butler-Sloss, L J (1988) *Report of the Inquiry into Child Abuse in Cleveland 1987*, HMSO, London

Carver, V (ed) *Child Abuse: A Study Text*, Open University Press, Milton Keynes (out of print)

DHSS (1974) *Report of the Committee of Inquiry into the Care and Supervision Provided in Relation to Maria Colwell*, HMSO, London

DoH (1995) *Child Protection: Messages from Research*, HMSO, London

Kempe, R S and Kempe, C H (1978) *Child Abuse*, Fontana/Open University Books, London (out of print)

Leach, P (1994) *Children First*, Penguin Books, London

Reder, P, Duncan, S and Gray, M (1993) *Beyond Blame: Child Abuse Tragedies Revisited*, Routledge, London

2

The Statutory Child Protection Framework

UNDERSTANDING ABUSE

Definitions

It is important to be clear that when we act in child protection, we act as agency representatives, not as individuals. This may legitimately limit our area of action but also places us under certain obligations. We may have all kinds of personal feelings about children, parents, families, relationships, etc. We may have many concerns about acceptable standards of childrearing or the kind of lifestyles we consider inappropriate. We may have certain political or religious objectives and ideals. While significant, these judgements are *not* the focus of our professional activity (or they shouldn't be).

This is difficult when, for example, a teacher is unable to persuade a social worker to take any action about a child or young person whom they consider to be at risk but others do not, or when a social worker insists on proceeding when the teacher is unsure. 'Good enough parenting' may *not* seem good enough to a teacher concerned about a child who sticks out like a sore thumb relative to their peers in the class and the general culture of the school, but who is quite 'normal' from the wider perspective of the SSD or health visitor.

'Moral danger' represents another common area of misunderstanding. For a teacher this may be a very significant issue, from the context of a duty to teach about relationships within a certain moral framework. To the social worker, the concept has no legal meaning, except where an assault is being alleged or a clear threat identified which places the child at risk of 'significant harm'. It has to be more than a matter of personal disapproval.

There is, however, another dimension to this requirement. Operating within agreed definitions and predefined roles, rather than feeling that this is something which we each have to resolve for ourselves in our own way, provides a certain amount of personal security and shared responsibility. As has been suggested already, while there is not necessarily an absolute consensus over what is meant by 'child abuse', there is a general sense of agreement among professionals and agencies about what kinds of actions towards children constitute the areas of common concern and what we must do about them.

Article 19 of the UN Convention on the Rights of the Child gives an internationally recognized agenda for both abuse and its prevention:

> 1. States Parties shall take all appropriate legislative, administrative, social and educational measures to protect the child from all forms of physical or mental violence, injury or abuse, neglect or negligent treatment, maltreatment or exploitation, including sexual abuse, while in the care of parent(s), legal guardian(s) or any other person who has care of the child.
>
> 2. Such protective measures should, as appropriate, include effective procedures for the establishment of social programmes to provide necessary support for the child and for those who have care of the child, as well as for other forms of prevention and for identification, reporting, referral, investigation, treatment and follow-up of instances of child maltreatment described heretofore, and, as appropriate, for judicial involvement.

A frequently used British definition is as follows: 'A child is considered abused or at risk of abuse by parents when the basic needs of the child are not being met through avoidable acts either of commission or omission' (quoted in the Staffordshire ACPC handbook).

This definition makes a number of points:

- Abuse includes the risk of it.
- It relates to basic needs.
- It involves actions by parents (and other carers).
- It relates to avoidable acts (ie, it excludes the effects of factors like poverty or poor housing).
- Abuse may involve deliberate actions or failures to act.

These criteria are not entirely the end of the matter. Some people question whether abuse should relate only to parents/carers, which is a major defining characteristic of local authority procedures. (Child Protection teams do not normally investigate children who are bullied or who are injured in dangerous sports, for example.) There is grow-ing awareness of a small number of cases involving abuse by other children and young people both within families and in residential care settings as well as new opportunity for computer-based child pornography through the Internet. There also appears to be an in-crease in extreme situations in which parents take their children's lives and then their own. Too much emphasis on the 'normal' pattern of abuse may mean that other kinds of incidents are unwittingly overlooked.

Some definitions focus more on the common characteristics of abusive behaviour: the misuse of power, the betrayal of trust and the lack of consent by the child. These approaches, in particular, help in identifying 'institutional' forms of abuse, for example, in residential schools, and are particularly relevant for sexual abuse. Others include reference to the social context in which the abuse is defined, recog-nizing that there has to be an element of general cultural/legal sanc-tion or violation of widely accepted taboos for a given behaviour to be classed as 'abuse'. Yet others stress the importance of persistence rather than 'one-off' outbursts of temper.

Categories

The primary categories of abuse are well known:

Physical injury
This includes bruises, lacerations, burns, fractures, eye injuries, etc. Recognition is a major issue here. All children have cuts and bruises from time to time. Clearly other factors also have to be taken into account: the frequency with which the child presents as injured; the younger the child, the more the injury should cause concern; signs which are consistent with biting and finger-tip bruising, especially in fleshy areas such as thighs or upper arms; and marks showing the outline of an instrument which may have been used like a stick, hairbrush or belt. Cigarette burns or scalds, especially to the hands and feet may also arouse suspicion. Teachers are *not* expected to be experts at diagnosis; even an experienced child protection social worker will not rely on their own judgement to determine whether a child has been abused. A professional medical opinion is essential. (Included more recently under this heading is poisoning and the deliberate harming of children to gain attention – 'Munchausen's syndrome by proxy'.)

Neglect/failure to thrive
This can be even more ambiguous and is often related to the expectations which agencies have of how children *should* be cared for. Neglect may be a sign of something more seriously wrong; a general breakdown in care at home, or long-standing failure to meet the child's basic needs. As far as possible, judgements should be made against mean objective criteria such as growth milestones, weight, etc. Children who are poorly clothed, hungry when they arrive at school, unwashed or without proper provision for their sanitary needs could also be included. Failure to ensure that the child has appropriate medicals might be a warning sign, though it is important to remember that very caring parents can still make mistakes and miss appointments or have objections to immunization, etc. Again, seeing the concern against the context of what is already known may be helpful.

Emotional abuse
This phrase is intended to identify those children who are not physically hurt but are brought up in an emotionally bruising environment in which their needs are met with hostility, indifference or verbal abuse. These children may regularly be ridiculed or shamed, subject to a humiliating role within the family or under constant threat of injury even if it never actually happens. They will lack any self-esteem and will often be seen as naughty or with behavioural problems. They may, however, be obsessively good at school – always anxious to please for fear of the consequences. They may give hints of being locked in their room at home or left on their own for long periods. They are 'starved' of affection and may be excessively clingy with other adults (especially younger children). This may be a process which has lasted many years and is often very difficult to isolate on its own. Basic needs like food might be conditional on their behaviour or one child in a family might be singled out as different and ostracized, perhaps where parental relationships have changed so that not all children are seen as equal in status.

Sexual abuse
This involves the participation of children in sexual activities which they do not fully understand, to which they cannot give informed consent or which violate either the law or social convention. Sexual abuse, whether of children or of adults, essentially involves an inequality. It is an abuse of trust or of power. It includes not only touching, penetration and other sexual acts, but also requiring the child to behave sexually, act as a source of adult sexual stimulation or participate in experiences which are age-inappropriate. Sexual abuse

usually involves 'grooming' – preparation for the abuse rather than being a spur-of-the-moment assault. Exposure to pornography or forced viewing of sexual activity between adults may also be included. Opinion is divided over the extent to which some sexual abuse may have a 'ritual' or organized element as part of its context/justification for the abuser. Boys as well as girls may be involved. The signs can be many and varied, from psychosomatic complaints and a general mistrust of adults, through to gross physical injury or pain in the genital/anal/abdominal area.

At risk of abuse
This concept does not appear as a category on a child protection register but I have included it to make it clear that assessing the risk of abuse is a crucial task of child protection as well as responding to abuse which has already happened. Many child protection procedures now use some form of 'risk analysis' which attempts to quantify the extent to which a child may be in need of protection, and from which kinds of abuse. The concept of 'dangerousness' is growing as a way of identifying those most at risk. This is actually the key issue in whether a child needs to be on a child protection register. Registration is only needed for children who are not yet safe and so need continued protection. This may also now be referred to as 'likely significant harm' in line with the concepts of the Children Act 1989 outlined in the next section. (The category of 'grave concern' is no longer used.)

How much abuse is there?

Much depends on the criteria which are applied. Some research has suggested that up to 60 per cent of women and 25 per cent of men have experienced some form of sexual abuse before the age of 18, though this requires a very wide definition. An NSPCC survey in 1995 reported that one in six adults has encountered some form of 'sexual interference', though there were questions about the validity of these findings. The Department of Health (DoH 1995 op cit) talks of 350,000 children at any one time who live in 'low warmth/high criticism' environments (a phrase which is growing in popularity).

Few, however, would put the level of actual abuse this high and such figures are in danger of obscuring the real issues for child protection as opposed to the wider concept of 'children in need'. The most significant figures relate to those children admitted to child protection registers (see Table 2.1). This is not, therefore, a measure of how many children are abused or even of all those cases which are reported. There are approximately 160,000 referrals each year, only two-thirds of which result in any further action. Many of these concerns will be entirely unfounded, and not all cases where problems are identified continue under child protection procedures.

Table 2.1 *Child protection case conferences (England)*

	year ended March 31st			
	(1991)	1992	1993	1994
total number of children on registers	(45,300)	38,600	32,500	34,900
rate per 10,000 children	–	35.4	29.6	31.7
new registrations during the previous year	–	24,500	24,700	28,500
children removed during the previous year	–	31,300	29,400	26,200
number of children who were the subject of a case conference during the previous year	–	40,750	42,600	45,800

In March 1994 there were 34,900 children on registers in England (31.7 children in every 10,000). This number had been falling in previous years (from 45,300 in 1991), largely in response to a general move towards less statutory intervention, but then rose again in 1993–94. This does *not* mean there have been similar changes in the levels of abuse. Referrals have been rising year on year (from 1,483 in 1991–92 to 1,962 in 1994–95 in Staffordshire, for example), and so has the number of child protection case conferences being held.

A total of 45,800 children were the subject of a case conference in 1993–94 in England, of whom 28,500 were registered. 26,200 were removed from registers in the same period. About 80 per cent of registrations each year are of children being placed on the register for the first time. About 70 per cent of registered children are under 10; with about 55 per cent girls and 45 per cent boys. About 25 per cent of registrations are for neglect (or as the primary category where there is more than one area of concern); another 25 per cent for sexual abuse; 40 per cent for physical abuse and 10 per cent for emotional abuse (DoH, 1995, op cit).

As has already been said, recognizing abuse is a source of concern to many teachers, but, in its fullest sense, it is not their responsibility. It is important only to know which incidents, injuries or reports from children are sufficient to raise concern. It is not for teachers to carry out the task of determining which children have been abused and in what way. Chapter 3 spells out the school's task in more detail, but at this stage it may help to be aware of questions like these:

- Could this have been an accident? Is there evidence of a recurring sequence of accidents beyond what would normally be expected in family life?
- Is the nature of the injury consistent with the reasons given? Does the child's/parent's explanation ring true; are there inconsistencies in the accounts?
- What is known already about the past history of care?
- Is the child developing normally; is the incident/concern out of the ordinary?

There are no guarantees of getting it right every time. The chances are that there is more abuse than we ever know about, but we do not know how much more. Children are capable of sustaining horrendous injuries accidentally or may do highly dangerous things without any lack of care by their parents. None of these questions can provide *evidence* of abuse and they should not be seen as doing so.

However, abusers can be very effective at providing plausible explanations; vigilance and common sense must come into play. Research has suggested that abuse is not restricted to one class or social group, and not only to those families who have always been seen as a 'problem' in the past. In that sense, it may be reasonable to be equally suspicious of everybody! I often say in my own training that child protection can be an issue for 'any child, in any school, at any time' just to make the point.

Causes of abuse

Why does child abuse occur? There are, of course a number of explanations. The following range is based on that outlined in Charles and Stevenson (1990, Part 2). It is a useful exercise to evaluate your own perceptions at this point. What relative weighting would you give to these various explanations? This also helps in analyzing your expectations about what should be 'done' about children experiencing abuse and highlights some of the differences which may lead to misunderstandings between those involved in offering children greater protection.

Inadequate individuals

This locates the causes in weaknesses and failings in the child's parents/carers, often on the basis of predisposing characteristics which make these particular people more likely to abuse, with relatively little reference to their social context. This may also relate to the particular interplay between the adults and the characteristics of the child concerned. The focus is primarily psychological and behavioural.

Some see abusive behaviour as a form of mental illness or criminality; others focus more on the personality and unmet emotional needs of the parent which make them unable to handle the responsibilities of parenting effectively. Theories of 'cycles of abuse' fit in with this understanding in which people who have been abused as children are more likely to go on to become abusers themselves.

The focus for understanding the abuse will be on exploring the parents' own upbringing and the likelihood that they will be looking to the child to meet their own needs rather than being able to accept an appropriate caring role. The frustration inherent in this situation is likely to lead to violence and anger against the child for failing to live up to these expectations. Alternatively, the adult may see the child as a source of comfort and reassurance and so put them at risk of sexual abuse.

Dysfunctional families

This is more about relationships than about the individuals within them. The particular focus is on the family: this is where the problem is; this is where the solution must lie, not in changing the personalities of the people concerned. Families are understood as 'systems' whose organic interrelationships need to be understood in context, both within the family itself and as a reflection of wider relationships outside. Each person within the system, including the child, both affects and is affected by the behaviour of all the others. Causation of abuse is circular within the network, not passed on generationally as with the more individual model.

Systems need stability to survive. The abuse of children becomes part of the means by which the network is protected and balanced. The key issue is the *function* of the abuse; 'how does the abuse help to maintain the family's balance?', not 'what causes the parents to act like that?' Abuse is a symptom of the dysfunction, not the cause of it. Indeed, abuse may be seen, even by the child, as the means by which the family continues to function. A failed marital relationship may be sustained by scapegoating the child; children may collude with the abuser as a way of holding the family together. This can become particularly acute in some sexual abuse (the West case was a classic example).

Social pressures

This is not simply saying that adults abuse children because of the social circumstances within which they live and so the individuals do not carry any personal responsibility. But the focus is on the parents/ carers *context* rather than their psychological functioning or the inter- action between them. Situational stresses clearly contribute to the actions of otherwise 'normal' parents who may lose control or become frustrated and unable to cope with the demands of their children. Dealing with the underlying causes is just as important as dealing with the presenting symptoms.

The NSPCC carried out a survey in 1992 and found that over 50 per cent of parents admitted going 'over the top' in dealing with their children, including screaming, shouting and hitting. Eighty-five per cent thought that they were under more stress than in the past and issues such as poverty, lack of secure employment, debt, problems with relationships and poor housing were identified as increasing the sense of frustration and pressure. Helping parents to be more effective in managing their responsibilities without damage to their children, may be as much about ensuring that they are properly housed or that there is enough money to pay the bills as about dealing with any personal failings.

Other analyses take a more structural view. For example, some see marriage and the family as declining social phenomena and abuse as an indication of the inability of such institutions to adapt to changed social circumstances. Violence within the parent/child relationship may be seen as a reflection of violence within the wider culture and so it cannot be understood in isolation. The philosophy behind this approach is important in local authority procedures, only part of which will ever be about attributing blame and changing individuals. While the abuse may be a crime, its prevention will almost certainly involve wider questions of social context and practical family support if there is to be positive change for the future.

Gender and power issues

This is a more recent area of understanding, but crucial for a complete analysis. Abuse is 'gendered'. In sexual abuse, girls are more likely to be the victims and the perpetrators are (almost) universally males. Physical abuse is much more equal, but issues to do with who does the parenting (mainly women) and who does the 'disciplining' (often men) can still be crucial in understanding how the abuse has happened.

Questions of power have been referred to already as part of the basic definition of what constitutes abusive behaviour. Much abuse arises from an excess of what is otherwise considered 'normal'. If men expect, or are given, a role as dominant, demanding, etc this is more likely to lead to an expectation that physical or sexual abuse of less powerful individuals within the family is acceptable. Much of this analysis, though not all, comes from within the feminist movement which holds that the view of women as objects, and children as subordinate, inevitably creates a climate within which abuse is encouraged.

More equal roles and relationships, it is argued, in which stereotypes are resisted and *each* individual is given recognition as a person, are less likely to create potentially abusive situations. Unrealistic expectations of the 'perfect wife and mother' lead to feelings of frustration and depression among women, reinforcing their powerlessness and guilt and, therefore, the risk of giving expression to these feelings by abusing the children who are even further down the hierarchy.

Facing up to feelings

This brief resume of definitions and understandings is intended to stimulate thought, not to confuse with a bewildering range of alternatives which cannot be reconciled! I find myself accepting some of all these analyses but not necessarily all of any of them. Trying to draw lines around what constitutes abuse and why it occurs is a process which is never complete. This section began by making it clear that we must act according to agreed criteria, not on our own judgements and values. But it is also important to reflect on where we are; no one can approach the abuse of children without personal feelings. This work is not the same as delivering the national curriculum or planning next year's timetable. Even getting this far may have raised all kinds of emotions for the reader.

Teaching is a stressful enough occupation at the best of times. Part of the stress inevitably arises from dealing with these kinds of issues. No one could reasonably expect anything else. But it may help to step back and analyze our feelings; this should be a key element in training events. For those whose own past experience has included being the recipient of abusive behaviour themselves, there may be a particular need to seek personal support and counselling. Asking for help should never be seen as a weakness. Such experiences should not be seen as necessarily either equipping any individual for, nor excluding them from, effective involvement in child protection.

Most of us will be a mixture of some or all of the following:

- *denial* – because recognition may be costly;
- *guilt* – because we all make mistakes;
- *fear* – that we won't know what to do;
- *anger* – that people can do such things to children;
- *pain* – at the recognition of abuse in our own lives;
- *jealousy* – if we have to let another professional take over.

To do the job we will have to be prepared to understand ourselves a little more; to approach ourselves critically and put our reactions to the test. But teachers must also be knowledgeable, objective and informed and few have sufficient opportunity to become so. It is now time to examine both the law and how it is carried out in order to address these requirements.

THE CHILDREN ACT 1989

A new legal framework

The remainder of this chapter is in two parts. Firstly, a summary of the legislation which underpins child protection, especially the provisions of the Children Act 1989, and secondly, an outline of standard local authority Area Child Protection Committee (ACPC) procedures, in the light of the key volume of government guidance *Working Together* (DoH, 1991). Familiarity with this information is *essential* for all those involved in child protection in order to retain an appropriately interagency perspective.

The focus is not, at this point, on the specific responsibilities of educational professionals which will be addressed in the next chapter. Neither have I included in any detail the question of criminal offences and how abusers are dealt with by the police and the courts. Interesting though this might have been, my concern, as always, is primarily with protection rather than abuse and its meaning for offenders. (The probation service is the best place to look for further information on this area if you have a particular interest. Understanding abusers is, of course, a vital contribution towards understanding abuse and so increasing children's protection.)

The legal basis for the protection of children by statutory agencies is Part V of the Children Act 1989 (implemented in October 1991). All work under the Act, which covers both 'private' law issues (such as divorce and separation) and 'public' law; (care proceedings etc), is based on certain theoretical principles:

The child's welfare is the 'paramount consideration'
This is very much a reflection of the priorities identified by the Cleveland Inquiry. In practice, this means that intervention should always be based around the child's best interests. If, for example, a child is at risk from an abuser within the family, it may be best for the child to remain at home with other trusted carers, with the abuser going elsewhere, rather than having to adapt to a new foster home, new school, etc. (Schedule 2.5 of the Act allows for local authorities to assist an alleged abuser to find alternative accommodation, even with cash if it is necessary.)

Delay is likely to be prejudicial to the child and should be avoided
There is less evidence that this principle has been universally accepted. Local procedures following an investigation may move at some speed; but lack of resources can still mean unreasonable delay and the courts appear to be operating no more swiftly than before the Children Act. There is still a fundamental tension over the need for long (and extremely expensive) proceedings if justice is to be seen to be done, and the need to avoid uncertainty about children's care as quickly as possible. The hope of reducing delay is best seen in shorter court orders than before and more tightly timetabled proceedings.

Courts should not make orders unless it is clear that to do so would be better for the child than not doing so
In general, agencies will seek to meet children's needs by negotiation and agreement, only using the powers provided by the courts when absolutely necessary. This again reflects the concerns of the Cleveland report that the statutory powers were used excessively, though there are signs that, after an initial period following the implementation of the Act, the use of courts is now closer to what it was before. The number of both emergency and longer term orders is creeping up again.

Decisions should be made in partnership wherever possible
Agencies should create effective partnerships, not only with one another, but also with families. Parents are of key significance, but other members of the extended family should be given the opportunity to participate in problem-solving wherever practicable. Parents should have the opportunity to contribute to case conferences and be given all possible information, albeit limited if necessary, by the paramount concern to safeguard the child's welfare (see also DoH/SSI, 1994).

Children have a right to be consulted and listened to when decisions are being made about their lives
This is not the same as saying that children can always have what they want, but their views should be respected and they must be given every chance to be involved and informed of whatever changes are planned for them. Children of sufficient age and understanding who are therefore 'Gillick-competent' are particularly relevant in this context.

Children in need

Section 17 and Schedule 2, Part I of the Children Act give local authorities a general duty to take reasonable steps to identify those children who live in, or are found in, their area and who are 'in need'. (The law was framed in this way, in part, to deal with disputes in past tragedies about who was responsible for children normally resident in another authority's area.) Part I also sets out a range of services which should then be provided to help these children and their families, from support within the home, family centres and counselling to 'accommodation' away from home on a voluntary basis (the replacement for what used to be called 'voluntary care'). There has been some disappointment since the Act's implementation about how little progress has been made in developing services of this kind, largely due to financial constraints.

Section 27 imposes a general duty on *all* public authorities, including education, to work together in providing these services for children 'in need'. The underlying philosophy is that the welfare of children is best encouraged, wherever possible, by promoting their upbringing *by their families*. Intervention to remove children from their parents/carers is extremely rare and often proves not to be to the child's advantage. The fear of social workers taking your children away on the slightest pretext is wholly unnecessary, though many families in difficulty are still deeply suspicious of them and reluctant to seek help. (This is not helped by the media, especially fictional drama, constantly portraying sensationalized and out-of-date images.)

A child is 'in need' if:

(a) he is unlikely to achieve or maintain, or to have the opportunity of achieving or maintaining, a reasonable standard of health or development without the provision for him of services by a local authority;

(b) his health or development is likely to be significantly impaired, or further impaired without the provision for him of such services, or

(c) he is disabled. (s.17(10))

This is clearly open to some interpretation, though there is less dispute in the field of child protection than there is, for example, about whether children with special educational needs or whose attendance at school is poor, are also children 'in need' under the Children Act. The definition is a kind of passport to services which effectively defines the boundaries of agency responsibility. There is always a danger that this decision will be 'resource-led' rather than 'needs-led', but it will be crucial in determining whether or not a social services department accepts a given referral as falling within its remit. They are not responsible for dealing with *all* the problems which children and families may have.

'Significant harm'

Of equal importance is the definition of the grounds on which an authority can justify intervention in a family through the courts. This has clearly been a problem in the past and the Children Act moves away from listing specific situations, such as 'moral danger' or absence from school (both grounds for care proceedings until 1991), in favour of more general principles. (This is why children can no longer go into care for 'truancy'.) 'Harm' is defined as 'ill-treatment or the impairment of health or development' (s.31). The concept of 'development' is very wide-ranging and includes physical, behavioural, emotional, social and intellectual development.

Significance is determined with reference to what 'could reasonably be expected of a similar child' and includes the risk of harm as well as actual evidence of it. Various tests such as parental care, or the lack of it, the care likely to be given in the future and whether the child is beyond control are then required. All this can mean that *proving* that the threshold for unwanted intervention has been reached is far from easy. The Act has, in effect, stressed that authorities must justify their actions far more thoroughly than used to be the case. This may be the reason behind the apparent reluctance of a social worker to respond to your concerns, not a lack of interest.

Duty to investigate

Section 47 gives local authorities a further duty to investigate a child's circumstances where they have reasonable cause to suspect that a child in their area is suffering, or is likely to suffer, significant harm. They must then take the necessary steps to ensure that the child's welfare is safeguarded and promoted and decide what action is appropriate. This is the problem with suggestions that less emphasis should be placed on investigation; there is a *duty* to do it when concerns are raised. Other named authorities, including education, have a *duty* to assist the social services in such enquiries (s.47(9) and (11)).

Clearly this process requires that social workers, the NSPCC or the police are given access to the child in order that the assessment may be made. These enquiries will be carried out under local ACPC procedures (as set out below) and may involve cooperation by schools in facilitating opportunity for interviews/examination. Only in very exceptional circumstances would children be seen without parents' knowledge and normally this proceeds without difficulty. All statutory powers are rarely used, but if parents are obstructing the enquiries, the following options are available.

Child Assessment Order (s.43)

This was introduced during the passage of the Children Bill as a means of proceeding with minimal interference to the family; a kind of half-way house between voluntary and compulsory action. The idea was first mooted in the report 'A Child in Mind' which had examined the death of Kimberley Carlile in 1987. An application can be made to a court in order to obtain authority to proceed with an assessment where parents have refused to cooperate. This, in itself, will often be sufficient to resolve an impasse but, if not, a CAO requires the parent to produce the child for examination. It does not entitle the SSD to keep the child away from home, nor is there any change in parental responsibility. It lasts only for seven days. If the authorities wish to remove the child from home as a result of the assessment, other applications will then be necessary.

The use of CAOs is infrequent and is only needed where *all* those with parental responsibility are refusing to cooperate. (Only the consent of one such person is required to proceed voluntarily as they each have the right of 'independent action'.) Orders are intended to promote a multidisciplinary assessment of a child's needs, though the emphasis is primarily medical. There has been some speculation that CAOs might also be used where, for example, a parent is refusing assessment by an educational psychologist. This is unlikely as they are essentially for short-term assessments where the necessary evidence, for example, bruising, has to be obtained quickly. In exceptional circumstances, an order might contain a direction that the child may be kept in hospital overnight, but longer-term disputes about children's welfare would be better resolved by a s.8 specific issue order or even by care proceedings.

There is a key point here about the possible refusal of a child to be examined. Even when a court has made an order, a child 'of sufficient age and understanding' may not agree to be assessed; the court is no more powerful than a parent in overruling their objection. Those examining older children should satisfy themselves as to their consent and, hopefully, any likely objection will have been raised when the order was applied for. Most doctors would refuse even to consider examining such a child against their will, though this concept does not necessarily apply to younger children.

Emergency Protection Order (s.44)
An *EPO* also requires a prior application to a court (though an order can be made *ex parte* without the parents being present). This is a more Draconian intervention in that the applicant acquires parental re-sponsibility for the duration of the order and can therefore make parental decisions about the child and remove them from home. The application must pass the tests of 'significant harm' and that the order will be better for the child than no order at all.

In theory, anyone with an interest in the child's welfare can apply, though action by anyone other than a social worker is extremely rare. The applications last for a maximum of eight days, but can be renewed for up to seven more. Keeping a child from home longer would again require applications for further orders (eg, an interim care order). This timescale is in marked contrast to the pre-Cleveland position where 28-day 'place of safety' orders could become almost permanent through frequent repetition.

Parents retain considerable rights during these proceedings, another legacy of the Cleveland Report. They may seek to have the order discharged or to obtain contact with the child. They do not actually lose their parental responsibility, though, in practice, it can be significantly curtailed. The orders are far shorter than before. Parents must be told what is going on and, after no more than 15 days, the authorities must be able to produce sufficient evidence to convince a court that the child is still suffering or at risk of signifi-cant harm or the child must be allowed to go home. There should be no more examples of children being kept away from parents without justification.

Police powers (s.46)
It is often not appreciated that the police have far greater powers than social workers, not only powers of entry to people's property but the right to remove a child in an emergency without any prior application to a court. This power is often referred to as a 'Police Protection Order', but this is a mistake, as no order is involved. A 'constable' may, at any

time, remove a child into police protection, or prevent a parent removing them from, for example, a hospital. They can use force to do so (s.17 Police and Criminal Evidence Act 1984), though this is rarely necessary. This is the power that enables the police to hold on to young people found in London railway stations or break into someone's home where children have been left alone in the middle of the night. It is not the social worker who can do this.

The police must tell the local authority and ensure that the child is removed to their care and parents informed of their action within 72 hours. In practice, this usually happens much more quickly. If necessary, the social services can then apply for longer term orders if the child should not return home or may accommodate the child with the parents' agreement. This is the 'easiest' way in which action can be taken, when courts are not in session and the situation is urgent. The spirit of the Act, however, requires the circumstances to be very unusual. There are also powers under s.50 for courts to make a Recovery Order where a child subject to an Emergency Protection or Care Order has been abducted, has run away or is missing.

Care Proceedings

Only a social services department can initiate proceedings to put children into 'care' or place them under a supervision order (s.31) longer term. Only a court can decide that the grounds are satisfied. This is quite different from the decision to 'accommodate' a child on an entirely voluntary basis (s.20) as a support to the family, and the status of the children involved should not be confused. Only for children 'in care' does the local authority acquire parental responsibility. Care orders give the local authority power to restrict the extent to which a parent can exercise *their* parental responsibility, though it is not entirely removed from them as under previous legislation.

The hope, in all but a very few cases, will still be to rebuild family relationships, not to end them. The grounds are solely the fact, or the likelihood of 'significant harm'. Care orders can be made on an interim basis: initially for no longer than 8 weeks; subsequent interim orders for no longer than 4. This is all designed to ensure that children do not stay away from home unnecessarily and that irreversible decisions are not made without proper scrutiny. Eventually, courts may agree that family relationships have entirely broken down and make a full care order, though children are often returned home while under the protection of the order. A few may be placed for residential, foster care or even adoption in very unusual circumstances.

AREA CHILD PROTECTION COMMITTEE PROCEDURES

An interagency perspective

All attempts to protect children adequately, in both the early stages of investigation and response and through longer term care plans, require effective working together between agencies. As has already been seen, this has been a repeated conclusion of the various inquiries which have examined why things have gone wrong in particular cases. All child protection work should keep this perspective in mind at all times, in both training and casework. There are sometimes difficulties about confidentiality, boundaries and respective roles which have to be explored at the local level, but awareness of the general principle is essential.

All child protection services are built around the key document *Working Together under the Children Act 1989* (DoH, 1991). This lays down general guidance about procedures which will then be defined in more detail in the handbook used in each local authority area. In each area (county, metropolitan district, or London borough), there is an Area Child Protection Committee (ACPC). Some large authorities are divided into several. These bring together senior representatives from a range of core agencies.

Social services
Often this includes the director, child protection specialists, etc. Social services carry the lead responsibility for the investigation and management of abuse and supervise the child protection register.

Health
This consists of paediatricians, nursing advisors, senior health visitors, child and adolescent psychiatric specialists, etc. Where there is more than one health authority/Trust within an ACPC area, there can be a large number of health professionals involved from both hospital and community services.

Police
The Police have increasing numbers of specialist officers who may work only in child protection. Their work is primarily in the early stages and in the collection of evidence for any possible criminal proceedings. They are not usually involved in the more child-centred work of protection, though they do have a key role in prevention including presentations in schools.

Education

Local Education Authorities will be represented by senior staff from within the education welfare/education social work service or by staff from within the special needs service. There are usually places on ACPCs for headteachers as well, as increasingly, LEAs alone cannot claim to represent all the local establishments in their area.

Other agencies

This might include the probation service, the voluntary sector such as the NSPCC, and other specialist groups, etc.

The ACPC carries executive responsibility for all child protection services in its area, the establishing of procedures and their regular monitoring, identification of significant issues arising from day-to-day casework, effective resourcing of both practice and training, promoting interagency liaison, and dealing with special review cases (following deaths or serious injury). If things are going wrong, the ACPC will need to be learning from the mistakes and their work forms a key part of local authority inspections by the Department of Health. ACPCs publish annual reports, copies of which should be available to schools as required.

The child protection process

What happens if there is concern about a child who may have been abused or is at serious risk? This procedure may not quite be universal, but any authority will be doing something very similar (see Figure 2.1):

Investigation

Investigations take place under s.47 of the Children Act in response to referrals, which may come from children and families themselves, relatives, neighbours or anonymous sources as well as professionals in contact with the child. The investigation has several functions:

- to establish the facts about any situation which has been referred or which has given rise to concern;
- to establish a record of the allegations being made or the evidence which is presented; what abuse has occurred, and over how long a period, etc;
- to make an assessment of current risk to the child;
- to establish whether there are continuing grounds for concern and whether protection procedures should be invoked or other services offered.

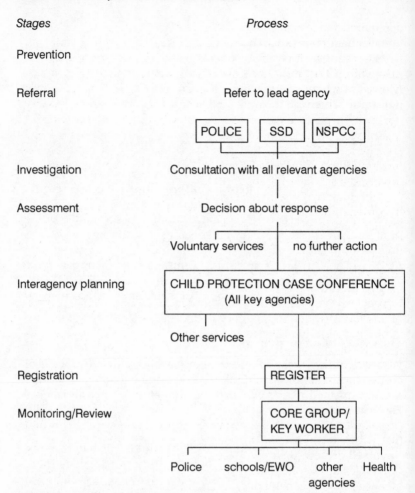

Figure 2.1 *The child protection process*

Thus the primary concern is not to identify the alleged abuser and to deal with them. This will be the principal role of the Police in joint investigations; the concern of social services will be to focus on the needs of the child. Investigation by specialist child care social workers, will normally involve making contact with parents and then with the child if this has not happened first, as well as any other key individuals in the child's life. It may also be necessary to consider the needs of other children within the household or to contact parents currently living apart from the family. Medical examinations will be arranged if required and formal interviews held, where children are old enough to talk about their experiences.

Interestingly, the report from the Social Services Inspectorate (DoH/SSI, 1994), indicates how much children dislike being interviewed at school, even when that is where they have first disclosed the abuse. There is a warning about being over-hasty in using school for such purposes; children feel that they have lost their privacy and parents feel publicly humiliated by having to address the issues there. Teachers may also feel that this can place them in an impossible position (though there can be no pretending that they have not been involved if school is the source of the referral).

Joint interviews by the SSD and the police are increasingly being recorded on video in accordance with the provisions of the Criminal Justice Acts 1988/1991 and the Home Office Memorandum of Good Practice 1992. This is in order to obtain evidence for any subsequent criminal proceedings. Interviews usually take place in specialist centres with toys, etc known as 'video suites' in which children can feel as much at home as possible. This avoids the need for the child to repeat their story again in court if the case comes to trial, perhaps many months later, though they do have to be available for cross-examination, ideally via live video link. Most recordings are never actually used (though many lead to guilty pleas) and there is some criticism of their value. It is extremely rare for children to be interviewed without their parents' knowledge and consent.

As explained earlier, the investigation process will also involve collecting as much information about the child and family as possible from other professionals. Social workers operate by a standard checklist which enables them to build up a picture from those already involved or from their own records. This should happen very soon after referral. Despite some worries about appropriate confidentiality, agencies have a general duty to assist the local authority and would be expected to do so (even during school holidays, if necessary).

Should the need arise, immediate steps will be taken to protect the child, nearly always on a voluntary basis, while further investigation is undertaken. This may involve placing the child elsewhere within the family or with alternative carers, or if required, encouraging the alleged abuser to leave the home. In some cases it may be necessary to apply for urgent orders. There will usually be a joint strategy meeting between key professionals at some point in the process, often before deciding whether to initiate a full-scale response. Once the immediate work has been done and an initial assessment made (if there are significant grounds for concern), the next step will normally be a formal case conference involving all interested agencies.

Case conference

If considered appropriate, *Working Together* recommends that a case conference should be held within eight working days of the referral, though it is often rather longer in practice. Social services are responsible for calling them. Conferences are not a forum for deciding that a child has been abused and who has done it; that is a matter for the courts, if necessary. Again the emphasis is on the child and their needs and the essential purpose is to provide a focus within which future work with the family will be agreed and coordinated.

A conference will be called:

- when there is evidence or high suspicion that a child has suffered, or is likely to suffer, significant harm; or when there is doubt about the situation and more information is needed to make a decision;
- when a child is known to be living in a household which contains an adult with a previous conviction of offences against children (known as a 'Schedule 1 offender');
- when there is concern about a child in a household where another child is already on the register;
- when a registered child moves into the area;
- when there is further concern about a registered child;
- when there are problems or disputes about the implementation of a previously agreed plan, or major changes in a child's circumstances;
- when requested by a key agency;
- when it is proposed to de-register a child.

Conferences require a range of agencies to be present, usually at least three, before decisions can be made. Most of the time they centre around whether a child needs to be on the register and what provision should be made for their continued protection. Increasingly, they are chaired by specialists from outside the directly participating professionals. Parents will normally be invited to attend, at least for some of the time, or be given the opportunity to express their views through their representative. This should also be true of children where old enough to do so. Invitations will be circulated to all potential participants, often at very short notice. If unable to attend, reports should be submitted in writing if at all possible. Minutes are also circulated subsequently and must be regarded as *highly confidential*.

The following checklist is recommended by the DoH as the information which is required *in advance* for all those invited to a case conference. This probably rarely happens, but it provides a useful reference point if there are problems which need to be addressed:

- the name of the person chairing the conference and relevant information about his or her task;
- the concerns which have led to the conference being called;
- information about child protection conferences, including their legal and procedural basis;
- the tasks to be accomplished and the decisions to be made;
- what the consequences of the conference might be;
- how the conference will be organized;
- information about the definitions of abuse and criteria for registration;
- information about the local ACPC procedures;
- information about any exclusion from all or part of the conference and the reasons for this;
- who will be present and why each person will be attending;
- where the conference will be held and how to get there;
- a copy of the agenda for the conference. (DoH/SSI, 1994, para.7.10)

This list is in the context of the information required by parents in order for true partnership to be reflected in the way in which agencies work. It is expected that this will all be explained to them before the meeting. However, the guidance also says that *all* participants should expect at least the bulk of this information in advance, though they will often not get it. I would argue at least for full details of why the conference is being called and what role might be expected of the teacher, EWO, etc. There may be decisions to be made about conflicting priorities or who is the best person to attend. This is impossible if there is little more than a child's name to go on.

Most case conferences now operate to a standard agenda. This is roughly what you would expect to find:

- introduction of those present (names and agency or relationship to the child);
- identification of key people who are absent/apologies;
- an outline of the purposes and aims of the conference;
- the 'ground rules' (confidentiality, etc);
- clarification of any missing information;
- reports about the incident/areas of concern and the result of the initial assessment;
- additional information from other agencies;
- comments by the family/child (if appropriate);
- consideration of the degree of risk to the child;

- decision whether or not to put the child's name on the register;
- recommendations for future work;
- appointment of keyworker and core group;
- date for review.

The child protection register

Children judged still to be at risk will be admitted to the formal child protection register. Only a fully quorate conference can make this decision and *all* professional participants should be invited to express a view. This procedure is as much about the perceived risk of future abuse as a measure of past abuse. It is always preferable to ensure children's safety without the need for registration. However, as has been seen in Table 2.1, there are signs that the numbers on registers are going up again as a way of demonstrating the scale of the problem and in order to secure scarce resources. Registration is essentially about *unresolved* needs and the proposed ways of dealing with them.

The register also provides a central record of children known to be at risk so that professionals who are concerned about an individual family can check their current status. Access is usually restricted to senior officers, including headteachers and senior education welfare staff, but making this check is an essential part of everyone's responsibility. (Enquiries are dealt with on a 'call-back' basis to ensure that confidentiality is maintained.) The register is held by social services and maintained on computer. It should also indicate under what categories the child has been registered and the position should be regularly reviewed.

The register should contain:

- the child's full name (and any aliases/known by names);
- address, sex, date of birth, ethnic and religious group;
- full names of those who have care of the child, together with information about who has 'parental responsibility' as defined by the Children Act;
- details of the child's family doctor;
- school, playgroup, etc where registered;
- categories under which registered;
- date of registration;
- name and address of the key worker;
- date when due for review;
- legal status of the child (any orders which affect the parents' rights, etc).

A record should be kept of inquiries to the register so that a pattern of concerns from individual agencies might become apparent to the 'custodian' or keeper of the register. If there are any changes to the child's address, school, etc it is essential that data is amended and key agencies informed. This does not always seem to operate as efficiently as it should. Procedures will also exist to deal with situations where children go missing, where there is a major incident affecting a registered child or when the child moves to another authority.

Core group
If there is to be continued action to protect the child, the conference will usually appoint a small group of professionals, under the leadership of the social worker (key worker). This group will be responsible for drawing up a detailed child protection plan and a more thorough assessment may also be undertaken. The core group should:

- identify the roles to be undertaken by each lead agency;
- set time limits and the timetable for reviews/meetings;
- clarify any obstacles to effective communication;
- define contact arrangements with the family (taking into account the wishes of the child and the parents);
- make provision for what should happen if things do not work out as the plan requires.

Reviews and deregistration

Reviews should be held at least every six months, to reformulate the child protection plan or to decide that the child can now be deregistered. Again, at least three agencies should be present for such decisions to be made. A child's name may be removed from the register for a number of reasons:

- the risk of abuse has receded within the family;
- the child has been placed away from home and is no longer considered to be at risk from the abuser;
- the abusing adult has left the household;
- the child has moved to another area which has accepted responsibility for their care;
- the child has reached 18, married or died.

It is essential to recognize that the decision to remove a child's name from the register, or not to register the child at all, does *not* necessarily mean that there is no need for services to the family on a voluntary basis. Continued vigilance may still be required and, while the child's safety may no longer be an immediate issue, there may still be considerable work to be done to enable the family to function appropriately or, occasionally, to assist the child in creating a new life within a new foster care/adoptive situation.

Special review cases (Part 8 reviews)

Additional procedures exist for those cases where there are deaths or serious injuries, together with incidents which arouse major public concern such as abuse within the public care system. This involves a review of existing files on the child by senior staff from *each agency*, and will also look at any concerns regarding siblings and other members of the family. Records must be secured immediately the request is made. A report on each such case now has to be sent to the Department of Health in order to establish that appropriate procedures have been followed.

These then are the general procedures and the legal framework within which educational professionals will be expected to operate. It is now time to consider the specific responsibilities of teachers and a range of related issues involved in creating appropriate policy for a 'child-protecting school'.

REFERENCES

Adcock, M, White, R and Hollows, A (eds) (1991) *Significant Harm*, Significant Publications, Croydon

Charles, M and Stevenson, O (1990) *Multidisciplinary is Different*, University of Nottingham, Nottingham (2 Parts)

Department of Health (1991) *Working Together under the Children Act 1989*, HMSO, London

Department of Health/Social Services Inspectorate (1994) *The Challenge of Partnership in Child Protection: Practice Guide*, HMSO, London

Russell, P (1992) *The Children Act 1989 and Disability*, National Children's Bureau, London

Wattam, C, Hughes J and Blagg, H (1989) *Child Sexual Abuse*, Longman/NSPCC, London

White, R, Carr, P and Lowe, N (1990) *A Guide to the Children Act 1989*, Butterworths, London

Whitney, B (1994) *The Children Act and Schools*, Kogan Page, London

3

The Child-Protecting School

GUIDANCE AND CIRCULARS

Meeting national requirements

The work of teachers in child protection is governed by a collection of documents, circulars and guides to good practice. None of them is enough on its own; they all have to be held together in order to appreciate the full picture. This can be very confusing for the busy teacher looking for one clear set of guidelines by which to work, but any thoughtful approach to the issues needs to take on board each of the following sources:

- *Working Together under the Children Act 1989 – A guide to arrangements for interagency cooperation for the protection of children from abuse* (Department of Health, Home Office, Department of Education and Science, Welsh Office, 1991).
- *Circular 10/95 – The Protection of Children from Abuse: The Role of the Education Service* (Department for Education and Employment). This replaced circular 4/88 from October 1995.
- *Paper 9 OFSTED Handbook* – From the Technical Papers in Part 5, together with Section 7.7 of the *Framework* on Pupils' Welfare and Guidance (May 1994).
- *Local ACPC and LEA handbooks* – local authority procedures together with any related guidance issued by the education authority.
- *Code of Practice and circulars on Special Educational Needs* – including sections dealing with the education of children with emotional and behavioural difficulties in the *Pupils with Problems* set (Department for Education 1994).
- *Bullying: Don't Suffer in Silence* – DfE Handbook (1994).

The need for policy

Together these cover the expectations of government and local authorities about the role of education staff in both protecting children and dealing with abuse. An addition was made to the draft of circular 10/95 which specifically requires that every school should develop a child protection policy and make it known to parents. Any school looking to act appropriately will want to make sure that governors, senior managers, pastoral staff, classroom teachers and every adult working within the school community has the right level of knowledge in order to be able to fulfil their particular responsibility. This does not mean that everyone has to be an expert; probably it is better to be clear that no one is, though senior management, in particular, should make sure that information is shared and procedures followed.

Some might assume that teachers are already well aware of their role and that no special policy is needed. Others might think that child protection is not a problem in *their* school and so no conscious effort is required to ensure that the issues are considered with any kind of priority. Both of these attitudes are dangerously misguided and, ultimately, mean that children may be put at unnecessary risk and their needs overlooked. Some recent research done outside the UK, but equally relevant here in my experience, is particularly informative.

Australia

A study of teachers (Johnson 1994), in six schools in South Australia, looked at the way in which a number of primary prevention programmes had been implemented in practice. During the 1980s resources had been made available to schools with a view to developing children's awareness about potentially abusive situations and how to deal with them. Many similar programmes exist in this country covering areas such as 'unsafe touching', helping children to assert their right to privacy, not keeping 'bad' secrets, etc. These, together with 'stranger danger' approaches, have been aimed at enabling children to protect themselves and giving them the necessary skills to seek appropriate help. (There is an irony in the fact that children are far more at risk from adults they know, despite high profile murders by strangers, which are extremely rare by comparison.)

Research into this process had already examined its impact on the children in generally positive terms; this study looked at how teachers had used it and what factors had influenced their approach. All the teachers had undergone preparatory training, but most had used only parts of the programme. The selection of which parts to leave out, however, depended primarily on the teachers' own feelings and experiences, not on the needs of the children. In effect, the teachers were editing down the programme and ignoring those elements which *they* found most uncomfortable.

The researchers acknowledge the agonizing these decisions caused; there was great concern for the children and much personal soul searching and even guilt about not delivering the whole package. There was, however, some collusion over avoiding awkward parts of the curriculum; a tacit agreement that personal memories might need to be protected and teachers' own sensitivities respected. There was little or no support or back-up provided to the teachers in order to help them to deal with their feelings together or individually. Colleagues tended not to talk about it or to 'interfere' in what were seen as private professional matters best left to the judgement of the individuals concerned.

The consequence was that children did not receive the information which they most needed. Crucially, while recognizing the importance of helping children actually being abused to 'tell' within the school community, there was much less agreement on the need for a more preventative approach. In short, this is a policy based on 'we'll do it when we need to', a very common response to child protection issues. It is not, however, enough.

Few of us do anything for which we are not fully prepared. Children may wait a day too long because we are not ready to hear them. I recently came across an example of a teacher who asked his primary class to list the dangers they face. It was his embarrassment, not theirs, which led him to write up 'naughty things' when a child specifically mentioned sexual abuse. This level of reticence is very worrying and would have discouraged any child considering disclosure. Good child protection practice requires effective preparation *and* appropriate response.

Ireland

Earlier research (Lawlor 1993), had looked at the awareness of primary school teachers about child sexual abuse and the likelihood of children being believed when they made a disclosure. The sample was 450 teachers in the Irish Republic. The general level of awareness was high in terms of knowing what sexual abuse is; though less so when it came to knowledge of those children most at risk (under 11s) and the generally young age of most abusers (between 15 and 35).

Male teachers were significantly less informed than female teachers; personal knowledge of someone who had been abused made little difference. There were considerable differences over the perceived level of sexual abuse (though, to be fair, there is no real agreement among the 'experts' about what percentage of the population has had direct personal experience), and a general understatement of the extent to which boys are as much at risk as girls. But at the level of knowledge, the respondents scored well.

When it came to believing disclosures, male teachers were rather more likely to be sceptical, though the overwhelming majority indicated that they would believe what the child said. The most interesting aspect of the study is what influenced teachers in this decision. The key issue was that they had previously *suspected* that a child in their class may have been abused (not necessarily the same child who was now disclosing). They were, in effect, prepared for the possibility, even if they had had no actual involvement in an individual case. In addition, those who had no personal anxiety about ever being accused themselves, were also more likely to believe a child when asked to do so.

These surveys suggest that there are three crucial areas to be aware of as we examine the guidance in detail. All of these should be borne in mind in the coming sections:

- Good practice in child protection must recognize the teacher's own feelings and offer strategies for dealing with them.
- Raising awareness, even when there has never been an actual case to deal with, is essential for creating the context for children both to disclose and be believed.
- Teachers are more likely to act appropriately when they are secure about their own position.

'Working Together'

This key document sets out the framework within which local Area Child Protection Committees plan their procedures. It covers some of the legal material in the previous chapter, but concentrates on promoting effective interagency working in both prevention and investigation. It is essential that school staff appreciate that they are core staff in this document, not on the periphery, but that their role is limited to certain key tasks. Neither under-involvement nor over-involvement is appropriate.

The guidance gives a brief indication of the role of each of the core agencies: social services, health, probation, the police, etc. The section on the education service (paragraphs 4.35 to 4.40) is reproduced below in full as it speaks quite clearly for itself. Following the quoted text, I offer a number of comments which link this guidance with circular 10/95 from the DfEE. I have added headings to each paragraph to indicate its content:

Role of education staff

The education service does not constitute an investigation or intervention agency, but has an important role to play at the recognition and referral stage. Because of their day-to-day contact with individual children during school terms, teachers and other school staff are particularly well placed to observe outward signs of abuse, changes of behaviour or failure to develop. Education welfare officers and educational psychologists also have important roles because of their concern for the welfare and development of children. Youth workers have regular contact with some children, and will therefore be in a position to help.

Awareness of local procedures

All staff in the education service – including those in grant maintained and independent schools, sixth form and further education colleges, and the youth service – should be aware of the need to alert the social services, the NSPCC or the police, when they believe a child has been abused or is at risk of abuse. They should refer cases according to locally established procedures. For the institutions they maintain, local education authorities (LEAs) should seek to ensure that all staff are aware of this and know what the proper procedures are. Social services departments (SSDs) should ensure that educational establishments not maintained by the LEA are aware of the local interagency procedures, and the governing bodies/proprietors of these establishments should ensure that appropriate procedures are in place, seeking advice as necessary from the SSD. For all educational establishments, the procedures should cover circumstances where a member of staff is accused or suspected of abuse.

Designated staff

The key element essential to ensuring that proper procedures are followed in each educational establishment is that the headteacher or another senior member of staff should be designated as having responsibility for liaising with SSDs and other relevant agencies over cases of child abuse. For establishments maintained by them, LEAs should keep up-to-date lists of designated staff and ensure that these staff receive appropriate training and support.

The child protection register

The relevant school, including nursery school, should be promptly notified by the social services department of the inclusion of a child's name on the child protection register. The details notified should include the care status and placement of the child, the name of the key worker and where possible what information has been made known to the parents about any allegations or suspicions of abuse. Schools will wish to pay particular attention to the attendance and development of such children and the designated teacher should report any further cause for concern to the social services department. The social services department should inform the school of any decision to remove the child from the child protection register and of the termination of a care order as well as any change in the status or placement of the child. The social services department should inform the school when a child who is already on the child protection register starts school. When a child on the child protection register changes school, the information should be transferred between schools immediately and the custodian of the child protection register informed.

Using the curriculum

Schools and further education colleges have a role in preventing abuse not only by adopting sound procedures on the management of situations where there is suspected abuse, but also through the curriculum. They can help pupils and students to acquire relevant information, skills and attitudes both to resist abuse in their own lives and to prepare them for the responsibilities of their adult lives, including parenthood. Some schools include specific teaching about the risks of child abuse and how pupils can protect themselves, within their personal and social education programmes.

National Curriculum Council guidance

A number of publications relating to health education and the development of a personal and social education curriculum are already available in schools and address issues related to child protection. More recently, the National Curriculum Council has advised that children aged five years and above should begin to develop skills and practices which will help them to maintain personal safety. It has also identified family life, sex and safety education as three key components of school health education, and has included family life education as a key topic in its advice to schools on education for citizenship. Its guidance to schools on both health and citizenship suggests ways in which these issues can be integrated into the wider curriculum and topics appropriate to different key stages.

DfEE Circular 10/95

This circular relates closely to *Working Together* and deals with both specific casework expectations and more general requirements. The following comments pick up on issues raised by both documents and *all* these points need to be taken into account for a truly comprehensive child protection policy:

Child protection is not an optional extra; it is a statutory duty on every LEA/school

This means it must be recognized, resourced and planned for. It is a matter of policy, not only of practice, and senior managers should ensure that the task is carried out appropriately (see Appendix 1). The circular specifically states that staff must be made available and supply cover arranged (for case conferences, etc) when the LEA advises that they are required. While the LEA carries the primary statutory duty, school staff are essential for an effective response.

All schools must have a designated senior member of staff
This should not simply be a name on a list or a paper exercise. Designated staff should be aware of their role, equipped to do it, recognized within the school and adequately trained. There may be uncertainty over whose responsibility this is in schools and colleges not maintained by the LEA; this must be clarified locally so that proper training is given.

Child protection is a whole-school task
All adults in the school community should feel part of the network of caring professionals. There is a real danger in off-loading the responsibility onto one person as if it were entirely up to them when it is actually everyone's job. This includes non-teaching and support staff as well as teachers.

Listening is essential but asking too many questions may hamper the investigation
Friendly enquiry is appropriate; interrogation is not. The evidence may be contaminated or there may be accusations that the child was 'coached' into disclosure.

Other professionals are available for advice
It is quite acceptable to discuss concerns (confidentially) with colleagues, both within and beyond the school, in order to make a decision about whether or not a formal referral is appropriate or to ascertain whether or not the case is already known. Not seeking help may be a significant indicator of a school which is under-prepared.

Local procedures must be followed
Copies of handbooks should be readily available, not locked away or their whereabouts known only to one person. (This was a major criticism of the school concerned in the Hunt report – see p. 96). I have often had to remind colleagues of the need to do what it says in the handbook. This is obvious but fundamental to good practice.

Grant-maintained schools and other non-maintained schools cannot 'opt out' of these responsibilities
There is some confusion about this as LEAs have a duty to treat all children in the same way, but are actually responsible only for schools which they maintain. *Working Together* says that the needs of other schools (including the independent sector), are primarily the responsibility of the SSD. GM schools and others should clarify the position locally and ensure that they are aware of who is available for help.

There may be local agreements which define responsibilities more clearly. The crucial thing is that *all* children are entitled to the same level of protection.

The efficient transfer of information on the child protection register is essential
In my experience this is often the weakest link in the chain: social workers don't pass on information to schools; schools don't pass it on to one another, etc. Confidentiality is not an excuse for inactivity when it comes to child protection. There must be effective, and confidential, channels of communication.

The curriculum offers several opportunities for the exploration of abuse and its prevention
This is a key way in which a school demonstrates awareness of these issues and promotes the prevention of abuse. Schools which do not give children the opportunity to explore these issues for fear of embarrassment or because it may suggest that the school has a 'problem', are putting children at risk unnecessarily. It also helps to create an environment within which it should come as no surprise to parents that referrals are made when concerns are raised. Schools which never mention child protection will find many more barriers than those which do (see also Appendix 2).

Allegations of abuse against teachers should be explored within a child protection context, not separately
(See Chapter 5 for consideration of this issue)

Bullying may raise child protection issues
(See below p. 70.)

OFSTED expectations

Child protection is mentioned at two specific points in the OFSTED handbook: in section 7.7 of the Framework in the section on 'Pupils' Welfare and Guidance' and in Specialist Paper 9. Both of these are integral to inspection of the school's pastoral care. The documents make it clear that inspection does not only relate to dealing effectively with individual cases, though this is essential, but also to a general sense of awareness and vigilance in order to create an atmosphere within which children feel safe and secure.

OFSTED basically expects all schools to comply with the guidance as above, summarized in Paper 9 as follows:

- There must be a designated member of the senior staff, responsible for coordinating action within the school, liaison with other agencies and monitoring local procedures.
- The school should be following the prescribed procedure for making referrals and discussing concerns with other key agencies.
- There must be effective monitoring of children on the register, proper representation at case conferences, submission of reports, etc.
- Child abuse/protection issues should be reflected in the curriculum in order to help children both to protect themselves and to prepare for responsible adulthood.
- Staff should be properly trained in order to increase their understanding and awareness of local procedures and enable them to recognize signs and symptoms, work with other agencies, etc.

Under the heading 'Effective Practice in Child Protection in Schools', Paper 9 also makes the following important points:

In the best practice, schools,

- have an ethos in which children feel secure, their viewpoints are valued, they are encouraged to talk and are listened to;
- provide suitable support and guidance so that pupils have a range of appropriate adults whom they feel confident to approach if they are in difficulties;
- work with parents to build an understanding of the school's responsibility to ensure the welfare of all children and a recognition that this may occasionally require cases to be referred to other investigative agencies as a constructive and helpful measure;
- are vigilant in cases of suspected child abuse, recognizing the signs and symptoms, have clear procedures whereby teachers report such cases to the school's senior staff, and are aware of local procedures so that information is effectively passed on to relevant professionals such as social workers;
- monitor children who have been identified as at risk, keeping, in a secure location, clear records of a pupil's progress, maintaining sound policies on confidentiality, providing information to other professionals, submitting reports to case conferences and attending case conferences;
- provide child protection training regularly to school staff and in particular to designated teachers to ensure that their skills and expertise are up to date;

- contribute to an interagency approach to child protection by developing effective and supportive liaison with other agencies;
- use the curriculum to raise pupils' awareness and build confidence so that pupils have a range of contacts and strategies to ensure their own protection and understand the importance of protecting others.

Finally in this section, it is worth noting the criticisms made in a joint OFSTED/Social Services Inspectorate report into the educational needs of children within the care system. Work with abused children does not end with referral and investigation. Some will need to live away from home and it is vital that schools cooperate in ensuring that educational disadvantage is not added to the problems they have already encountered.

> Teachers and social workers do not understand the requirements of care and education respectively with the result that there is little discussion of the educational needs of the children. Responsibilities for different tasks are not clear and the educational needs of individual children are not constantly addressed. Effective liaison also requires clear procedures for sharing information, but these are rarely developed. In addition there is a lack of appreciation of the expertise and role of other professionals.
>
> If the standards of achievement are to be improved, individual schools have to assume, in conjunction with the LEA a greater responsibility for fostering and maintaining the partnership with the SSD and developing strategies which promote the achievements of children. (SSI/OFSTED 1995, paras. 90 and 92)

The report is a fairly damning indictment of the way in which the needs of some of the most vulnerable children remain unmet. Not all the children studied will have been abused (other than by the system), but the survey illustrates that without a conscious effort to work more effectively together, good practice will not happen. These tasks are too important to be left to chance.

FROM THEORY TO PRACTICE

Teacher competence

All of these documents are helpful and must be familiar territory for any school wishing to take its child protection responsibilities seriously. There is enormous danger in school staff rushing into casework without sufficient thought about the limits to their role or believing that they alone can resolve the problems of a child alleging abuse. We must act within the guidance (so we must know it), and not only according to our instinct. My first advice to a headteacher unsure of how to proceed is sometimes to tell them to do nothing – for five minutes – and *then* read the handbook and decide what to do having distanced themselves from the situation and thought more calmly about it.

But guidance alone is not enough. Most of the skills required for child protection cannot be explained in a book; even a procedural manual is only much good when actually used. There is no substitute for practical experience. This book certainly should not be used in such a way. The key word in social work is 'competence'; professionals are expected to know how to do their job. Preparation for that task requires opportunities to explore the role through groupwork, interagency courses, case studies, establishing local networks, etc (see Appendix 2).

Training can be a problem for teachers. I have been heavily involved in recent years in devising and helping to deliver inter-agency courses on child protection. The whole approach is built around professionals becoming more familiar with both their own role and that of others. But how many teachers can be released for a two-day training course? Few other people are in the same position as teachers; there are far more of them than those in other agencies and it is much more difficult for them to be away from their normal duties. This can lead to teachers being trained only with other teachers and not with workers from different agencies; or, even worse, not being trained at all. This has many dangers, not least because the vital interagency approach to the task may not be fully explored.

Any training for teachers must be sensitive to this and at least be delivered by those representing other agencies, even if the participants cannot always be a similar mix. The intention of this section is to offer advice about actually doing the job. It reflects the kinds of comments which teachers have made to me on courses I have helped to run; but it is not a replacement for attending them!

Identifying abuse

This is probably the area that causes most concern. This is natural enough; the price of getting it wrong may seem frighteningly high and there is no guarantee that we will always get it right. I find that teachers are reassured even by this admission. Individuals sometimes imagine that they are the only ones who find this difficult; but even specialist social workers do not rely on their own judgement alone. When faced with a child who *may* have been abused, what realistic criteria can be applied which will at least ensure a reasonable level of confidence in one's decision?

I have avoided reproducing here a detailed checklist of signs and symptoms (but see also Chapter 2). These are usually available locally, and are included in the written guidance, but there is a danger with lists. A child may 'score' very highly on the various identifying characteristics without any real evidence that abuse is an issue. Indicators can never 'prove' abuse and can be misapplied. I prefer to encourage staff to rely on a combination of three things:

- experience
- evidence
- empathy.

As with the available documents, all of these must be held together; none is enough on its own. They depend on *the* most important thing in child protection – a quality relationship between the child and a trusted adult within the school community. (This does not have to be a teacher.) There is no chance of a child feeling confident enough to disclose, or of anyone feeling able to act on a concern, if the two people involved are strangers to one another. Referrals grow out of relationships, not out of an indifferent judgement that certain criteria have been met.

Not, of course, that there is no element of objectivity; there must be. But recognizing children who are at risk, who are being abused at this moment or who may have a history of abuse in the past, always requires an encounter between two individuals. More children first give rise to concern to a teacher than to any other professional. Sixty per cent of referrals for school-aged children come through schools. This is good news, not a burden. Even with all the current pressures on pastoral care, this essential element of school life, even for older children and young people, must never be neglected. If schools ever become places where children come simply for intellectual programming, this whole element of care will be lost forever and children will suffer the consequences.

In this context, experience, both of this particular child/family and of the child protection process, will enable us to be sensitive to those who need our help. Of course there is also the element of evidence; both what we see and, crucially, what the child is saying. But the *empathy* is paramount: the ability of the teacher to enter into the child's experience and to feel what they are feeling. This is not the same as 'sympathy': feeling sorry for the child or even sharing their sadness. It is about being there with them – 'walking in their moccasins'. My principal advice to a teacher who is not sure whether a child is being abused is to get to know them better; maybe the bruises or the story will make more sense then. The classic signs can be learned; the empathy has to be part of us.

Sadly, the signs of abuse are sometimes misinterpreted, and not primarily in the sense that physical injuries are seen only as innocent accidents. If anything, the reverse may be true, so anxious are we all not to miss a cause for concern. But probably of more importance is that behaviour in response to abuse may be misunderstood as 'naughty' or 'attention-seeking', or as 'typical of that family'. Abused and damaged children may misbehave; they may be at risk of exclusion or attend irregularly; they may not show the respect and obedience towards adults that we would normally expect.

We need the skill to see the behaviour as a symptom of the problem, not as the problem itself. Not, of course, that all naughty children are being abused, though evidence suggests that many abused children do exhibit their distress only indirectly. But again, empathy may help us to avoid jumping to conclusions; it should make us suspicious of stereotypes, more interested in making a judgement *about* the child than a judgement *on* them.

Consultation

If you are presented with possible abuse but unsure whether you have the basis of a referral, talk about the evidence with someone else, within the context of confidentiality outlined below. There should be support available from the LEA and within the school. Teachers often feel that they dare not ring the social services for fear of beginning an unstoppable process. This should not be the case. It is possible to ring for advice, talking in general terms without necessarily even mentioning individual names. It is usually, however, best to make the enquiry specific to a given child, especially if there is a past history of concern so that the register and other records can be checked.

Any decision to proceed should include a proper respect for the referrer's own professional insights, though the final say has to rest with the investigating agencies. Even at the risk of losing control in this way, it is rarely, if ever, better to sit on the little information you have and do nothing at all for fear that you will do the wrong thing. At the very least, share the issue with the school's designated member of staff or a colleague in another school. Above all, resist the temptation to wait until last thing on Friday afternoon and then contact others; this simply puts everyone under unnecessary pressure.

My suspicion is that schools which are best at recognizing and identifying abused and at-risk children also have effective pastoral systems; open and affirming contact with parents; well-trained and motivated teachers; clear and purposeful policies etc. It has to be part of a package. All schools claim to be caring communities. But the ideal needs clear signs that it is true in practice, and for *all* children, if it is to mean anything. An absence of any agreed policy and procedure for protecting children will make the individual teacher's task much more difficult.

Such schools have staff with time for one another when something needs talking over; children who are encouraged to be sensitive to the needs of other children; space within the life of the school for promoting personal development which meets the varied and individual challenges which the children pose. Some schools show this by setting counselling time aside; some have established peer support; some use volunteers or have prepared all their staff, including non-teaching staff, in basic listening skills. Of course it requires a commitment of scarce resources, but I am sure that such a programme is *the* most important factor in building effective systems of recognition and response.

Listening to children

Much of the time our first source of information about possible abuse will come from the child, as well as from our own observations. Even quite young children may feel sufficiently confident in their relationship with a teacher or classroom helper to say something to them. Older children may either be more easily articulate, or even less willing to put what they feel into words! Embarrassment is likely to be a greater obstacle for the teenager than for the 6-year old. Children with special needs, including those with linguistic and sensory disabilities, may require particular skills from staff able to pick up non-verbal cues.

Opportunities for children to speak to you; space within the day for sharing, doors which are open when someone is there to listen, will all help the child wondering whether *this* is the right time and place to say what's been on their mind for weeks. Dealing effectively with small problems will make it more likely that a child will trust us with a bigger one. If we cannot find time for the trivial they may assume that we are far too busy for something more significant.

At the point of disclosure or when our own concerns are raised, the alarm bells must start ringing in our heads. Training should prepare us to know what to do when a child wants to talk about something which we begin to feel amounts to abuse. Of course we want the child to talk to us; but we do not want to interrogate them, nor to put at risk the potential investigation and even criminal prosecution which may lie ahead. At the beginning, we do not know where it will all lead so *every* situation has to be treated as an example of the best possible practice.

The usual advice is about boundaries. As has already been said, teachers are not responsible for investigation and the fewer times the child has to repeat their story the better. The task is to obtain sufficient information to make a decision about where to go next. It may be obvious: 'My mummy's boyfriend has got a big snake that spits at me when I'm in bed. It always happens when she's out and I'm not allowed to tell her about it.' There is no need for *any* more discussion with the child; just comfort and care until the next stage of the process. It may be less clear: 'I don't like my mummy's boyfriend. He makes me do things I don't want to do.' Like tidying her bedroom or brushing her teeth!

Commonsense is a valuable ally, but not to be trusted entirely. Above all, avoid leading questions. Do not put ideas into the child's mind. ('Did he tell you to touch him? Does Dad hit you often?') Stick to 'That's a nasty bruise; how did that happen?' Do not ask the child to change what they have said. The primary aim is to give the child space. It is best not to interrupt, nor to seek too much detail unless it is really not clear what they are saying. It must be *the child's* story with no grounds for anyone claiming later that they were 'coached' into saying certain things by someone else. All you are doing is gathering what you need to make an initial decision; listening and then re-sponding to what you hear.

Writing things down

In very exceptional circumstances, the person who first hears the child's story may be asked, perhaps a year later, to give evidence in court about what was seen or heard. The defence barrister will try to find inconsistencies or accuse the teacher of making the child say what they wanted to hear. Or a child may be seriously injured and, as part of the investigation, the child maintains that they told a teacher several weeks before about a previous incident, but nothing was done. The teacher cannot remember it; another teacher then recalls seeing an injury about three months before, or was it some other child? Both of these situations would be best handled by keeping immediate written records. As you never know which cases may end up in this way, you need to keep records as a matter of routine.

This is also important if you decide *not* to make a referral at this point. This often happens. It is essential to record the fact that a concern was raised, a discussion held, a decision made to continue monitoring the child. I have come across several examples of schools, when faced with a sudden disaster, falling into a total muddle about what had gone on before or, worse still, contradicting both each other and the child about what has happened previously. Some feel that recording the decision to do nothing may be used against them in the future if there are grounds for concern; better to 'pretend' that we didn't realize anything was going on or keep it all 'unofficial' just in case. This is not acceptable.

It is wise to date and sign the report and to ask a colleague to witness that what you have written is contemporaneous to the events (the same day). It might be in a school log-book or on a child's personal file; it may be best to use a standard format (see, eg, NAHT, (1993)). Obviously it must be confidential. If anyone else discussed the matter with you, ask them to keep a written record too. Someone should be in a position to spot trends if, for example, a child has given three different teachers cause for concern in the last 10 days, even though none of them has spoken to the others. Take notes of any meetings with parents, telephone calls or related information. All of this may enable the decision over whether to refer to be made more quickly when the time comes without spending hours trying to piece together various bits of information which are only in people's memories.

Making a referral

It does not necessarily have to be the designated teacher who makes the referrals. If this is the headteacher by default (not an ideal arrangement), it is probably best if someone who has more direct contact with the child contacts the relevant agency. Ideally all teachers will have sufficient awareness to be able to act appropriately, if in consultation. Making a referral is always easier if you know the person to whom you are referring; opportunities for key staff from the child protection investigation team or the local social services area office/NSPCC/ police to visit the school will help the process to feel more comfortable.

Referrals, usually made over the telephone, and *confirmed in writing* (with copies to appropriate LEA officers and school medical services), should make it clear that the child protection procedures are being invoked, as distinct from a general enquiry. A referral must contain certain basic information.

- The child's full name, date of birth, address, ethnic and religious group.
- Details of other members of the child's family and those who live with them. (This is one reason why data collection procedures need to be kept up to date and store information relating to all 'parents', including step-parents etc.)

- Details of all those with 'parental responsibility' as defined by the Children Act 1989, including, in particular, any such person who lives apart from the child (another key area for data collection).
- Name and telephone number of the relevant GP and any other known medical information.
- Whether there are any court orders relating to the child (eg, section 8 orders under the Children Act and the current status of the child if already known to the social services).
- Where the child is at the moment and how long they will be there.
- Where parents are at present (if known).
- Where the referrer will be for the next few hours.
- What the referrer has seen or heard, descriptions of any injuries, what the child has said, past records of concern, etc.
- Any other information requested by the investigating agency.

Referrals need to be made at the right time – that is, not too early (when there is no real basis for concern) and not too late (when the information has been available for some time already). This also applies to the time of day or the day of the week. Referrals should not be made to clear the desk (or the conscience). They should be made when the child's needs require it and, preferably, early enough in the day for the social worker/police to be able to gather the necessary information, especially if the child will be safe at school for several hours before anything needs to be done to ensure their protection. Telling someone *after* the child has gone home is especially unhelpful. It is not good practice to keep children up late because interviews were not arranged early enough in the day.

Department of Health guidance (DoH/SSI, 1994 op cit), suggests that the need for referral should first be discussed with the family. This is not realistic in many cases, and in my experience, does not happen with most referrals that arise through schools. Teachers are nervous enough about this process already, if, for example the concern turns out to be misplaced or if the parent should immediately see the school in a hostile way. It is difficult to see how this idea can be reconciled with ensuring that parents are not 'tipped off' prior to an investigation and the general rule is *not* to contact the parents yourself without prior advice. Negotiating an appropriate sense of partnership with the family in the child protection process is not primarily the referrer's responsibility, not, at least, at this early stage.

Confidentiality

This has a number of facets in child protection work. As has already been noted, there may be a need to discuss concerns with others. This must be done responsibly. Schools are large communities in which it is often difficult to keep things secret. This must not be left to chance but deliberately managed. Gossip is clearly lethal in this context, but there are a number of other less obvious issues:

What if the child doesn't want me to tell anyone?
This can be very complicated. It depends on a number of factors: the age of the child, what they are telling you, etc. In general, there can be *no* assurance of absolute confidentiality. You cannot promise not to tell anyone else. You can promise not to tell anyone without the child knowing, or not to tell their parents or to tell them who you will tell about what. But you may be under a duty to pass the information on and, hopefully, the child can be reassured that you will stay with them and make sure that it all works out alright. (This is another point at which personal and professional feelings must be distinguished.)

The exception might be where the child is considered 'Gillick competent'; that is, 'of sufficient age and understanding' to decide for themselves what should happen. There is no fixed age for this; perhaps an average 14/15-year old is the best guide in this context. If such a child wants what they talk about to be kept secret, it might be appropriate that their rights should be respected. No one, for example, could force a teenager to be medically examined against their will; an investigation team is unlikely to proceed if the child is specifically telling them not to.

But children might be willing to talk to someone else and think about it further or be helped to see that there is a risk to a younger sibling as well which they cannot handle by themselves. Personally, I would still ask if I could discuss what they have said with someone else and ask for their advice. I would also keep a confidential written record even if the child asked for no further action to be taken, though some might say this is still an infringement of their right to privacy.

What about sexual activity?
The 1994 circular from the (then) DfE on sex education in schools (No.5/94) has muddied the waters by suggesting that headteachers should inform parents if under-age young people disclose that they are sexually active. What if the father is the sexual partner? – clearly a child protection referral, but maybe the young person will not want you to proceed for fear of the consequences. Is under-age sex sexual abuse? – probably not if the relationship is within conventional

boundaries and the young person is giving willing consent. Teenagers are entitled to confidential health care, including contraception, in their own right without parental knowledge, let alone consent if appropriate.

I doubt there is ever a reason for a teacher to pass such information on to parents without permission, and legal opinion has questioned the DfEE advice. It *is* important to encourage the young person to discuss it with parents themselves if at all possible. Acting as 'honest broker' might be helpful in giving the young person confidence to raise the issue at home. Clearly great caution should be exercised if it is the parent/step-parent/partner involved in the relationship (even a mother may be colluding). This is definitely an area for seeking advice locally and headteachers should not act unilaterally by contacting parents first.

What about data protection?
The Education (School Records) Regulations 1989, exempt informa-tion about child protection from having to be passed on to parents in the same way as other school records. Such data can be removed from a file which must otherwise be open for inspection. Guarantees of confidentiality, given under the Data Protection Act 1984, when col-lecting parental data for the admissions record system, can also be waived in the greater interests of the child, that is, by passing on names and addresses of parents, etc to other agencies if required.

This is not without difficulty and some parents ask for safeguards which we cannot give. In general, as indicated in Circular 10/95, it is best to be entirely open with parents *in advance* by making it clear in the school's policy that any concerns about a child's welfare will be passed on to the appropriate authorities if required. A statement to such effect could be included in the school brochure as part of the commitment to the pastoral care of the child.

In effect, a parent is asking you to act for them while the child is at school. Arguably, this can be seen as including acting to protect the child, even from those same parents if necessary. Being honest about this right from the word go may help to diffuse a situation where parents resent what the school has felt it must do. No school can promise that they would never do such a thing without their permis-sion, though social workers will nearly always seek to proceed with parental consent rather than behind their backs if at all possible.

Attending a case conference

As has been seen in Chapter 2, interagency conferences are often an essential part of planning the response following an allegation of abuse. For any school-aged child, teachers and other educational professionals are essential to the management of a child protection plan. Relationships do not always work as well as they might, but trying to work together from the beginning of the process increases the chances. The DfEE circular 10/95 draws particular attention to case conferences and the need for designated teachers and others to know how best to contribute to them.

There are real tensions here: pressures on time, cost implications and some conflict between the ways different agencies operate. Other people at case conferences sometimes seem to attend them so often and know each other so well that a teacher may feel de-skilled. Despite the intentions of the guidance, we do not always have the information we need to be able to ensure that the time will be well spent. It is clear that releasing staff to attend is normally a priority, in order to make a meaningful contribution to decisions. This is true for *all* schools, including grant-maintained schools, city technology colleges, the independent sector and colleges of further education.

Each participating agency is responsible for:

- preparing and presenting their own contributions including direct evidence, as far as possible in writing;
- being clear to what extent they can commit resources from within their own agency;
- contributing to the assessment of risk, both actual and potential on the basis of specialist knowledge, past experience etc;
- agreeing to and carrying through an appropriate role, including participation in a core group if appropriate;
- providing written reports if unable to attend in person.

Reports should show the evidence of good practice expected of any report to an outside agency. They must be based on objective facts not on personal opinion, give a 'rounded' picture of the child and indicate what role the school is able to play in continued work with the family. It is important to remember that, unless the circumstances are very unusual, reports will be shown to the parents and, where appropriate, to the child. This means there can be no hiding the fact if it is the school which has raised the alarm. Staff should feel confident in their role of 'safeguarding and promoting children's welfare' even if it sometimes means a conflict of interests with their duties towards parents. Case conferences may well expose underlying tensions.

It is best if the person attending the conference is personally knowledgeable about the child. This usually means the class teacher, year head or, in primary schools, the headteacher. It does not have to be the designated teacher every time; indeed, it is much better if the experience is not kept to one person. It must be clearly understood that attending the conference is only the beginning of a process, not necessarily the end. Those representing the school have a right to feel that if they are needed for future work, they will be released from other responsibilities to do it.

There may be some dispute about whether a case conference is needed. Most local authorities accept that an element of judgement must be applied and that resources do not always permit as many cases to go forward as *Working Together* implies. There is some concern about the number of investigations that do not result in further action (though this could be seen as good preventative practice). This should be a decision made according to clear criteria by a senior manager within the SSD, not simply something which is arbitrary. If concerns and referrals are not dealt with as anticipated, and local resolution has not been possible, LEA representatives on the ACPC or a local review committee should be asked to clarify the process. Services may, of course, be provided in some other way, without need for child protection procedures. This is always a preferable alternative if suitable.

Monitoring a child on the register/core groups

Finally, a word about the role of teachers where children are admitted to the child protection register and school staff are involved in the core group. For school-aged children, teaching staff are essential for good practice, and should usually be included. Social services are responsible for informing the school in writing that a child has been registered and who the key worker is. This information should be recorded on the child's personal file and, where confidentiality permits, on the individual student's database. It is essential that those who *need* to know are aware of the child's status and what it means.

Having a child in your school who is on the register involves certain responsibilities. It must be clear whose jobs these are:

- sharing information about the child within the school's pastoral care system;
- liaison with the key worker/social worker, especially about relationships with parents, what to do if the child is absent, any change of circumstances, eg, court proceedings or change of address/carer;
- liaison with other agencies, especially education welfare. (Many LEAs operate the system for informing schools of children going on and off the register through the Education Welfare Service);

- vigilance about the child's general well-being, attendance, any change of circumstances, general progress, etc;
- core group meetings, reports and follow-up;
- reviews of registration, etc.

Management issues (see also Appendix 1)

Ensuring that all this practice is in place is essentially the responsibility of senior management; staff and governors. Teachers are entitled to feel that this wide range of responsibilities is recognized and resourced and that policy for child protection is at the heart of the school's life and structure. There should be no question of 'dumping' these tasks onto individuals without a clear commitment to their importance for the whole school community. It is, after all, the Senior Management Team and the governors who are ultimately responsible for meeting the requirements of circulars, etc. They should at least share the responsibility of answering to OFSTED, or to the ACPC if procedures have not been followed. Appendix 2 contains some suggestions for governor training so that they can address these issues at policy level.

Feeding information back to managers about the work done in the school is essential, albeit within the limits of careful confidentiality, (especially where other parents are concerned). Some governors may be reluctant to see good practice in child protection as a sign of a 'good' school. There may be a feeling that 'this kind of school does not have those kinds of problems'. As with facing up to the reality of 'unauthorized absence' or children with special educational needs, there may be a temptation to try and keep potentially difficult children and their families out of the school in the first place or to pretend they do not exist.

This is wholly inappropriate and is evidence, not of a 'good' school, but of one with its head in the sand which is basically uninterested in children and their needs. Children are abused; it is a fact of life. Not all such children come from 'problem' families; you cannot always predict in advance who they will be. It could be my son or daughter at risk; it could be the most hard-working best-behaved child in the school. Of course there are pressures on time and resources, but I would not want my children at a school which was not prepared to help them when in trouble, nor ready to recognize their needs when required. *All* children are entitled to attend schools which are alert to these issues; it is as much a right as education itself.

BULLYING

Bullies and the bullied

Bullying is not usually seen as a child protection issue, except at its most extreme. Even schools committed to all the procedures we have looked at so far, which are designed to ensure that the school is vigilant and caring in response to incidents which happen within the family, may not see what is happening within the school in the same light. The existence of bullying as an issue may be denied; it may seem inappropriate to put alleged sexual abuse alongside a minor playground scrap; there may be a commitment to dealing with bullying only as a disciplinary issue without much understanding of what it means for the individuals involved.

Talk of bullying quickly raises issues about judgements, feelings and values. Here, as with child abuse in its conventional sense, we must be careful to distinguish our personal and our professional reactions. Just as teachers are anxious about being the subject of an allegation, they are also worried about violence from children, both from children against children and against themselves. There are a few children in our schools who are a positive danger to those who have to work with them. It may seem easiest simply to exclude them; to off-load the problem onto someone else or allow them to be absent without taking any action in response. While understandable, these are hardly acceptable as solutions.

There may be ambivalence about appropriate boundaries, just as there is over parental discipline. The culture of the school may emphasize toughness, even encouraging children (especially boys) to stand up for themselves. (This will, of course, be commonplace in the culture of many families anyway.) Teachers may feel powerless in the face of children who will not respond to reason. We may have clear ideas about the 'undeserving' nature of the bully in contrast to the 'innocent victim' who suffers at their hands. Bullying may be seen as a potential bad judgement on the school and so swept under the carpet. Or we may see it all as just a part of growing up and not really the responsibility of teachers at all.

Bullying as abuse

My thesis is that a school which is serious about child protection will also be serious about tackling bullying. It will recognize that bad things can happen to children while in our care which can be extremely traumatizing for them, not only in terms of physical injury, but also as emotional abuse. This can be seriously disruptive to children's education, threaten their mental health and even, *in extremis* cause them to try and take their own lives. No child should have to put up with violence from a peer, any more than they have to from a parent.

A good school will admit that bullying by pupils and by teachers is possible and face up to both. It will acknowledge that the way the school is run, the physical layout of the buildings or the structure of the school day may be part of the problem. It will see bullies as victims too, who are also 'children in need' and seek to ensure that *all* children receive the help to which they are entitled. Rather like the approach discussed so far, my emphasis is less on blaming than on protecting.

Clearly I am influenced, especially in seeing the needs of both the bully and the bullied, by my own experience. When I was 10 I was hit over the right eye by a large stone thrown at me in the playground. It needed several stitches (I still have the scar!). I was paraded around the school by the headmaster in order to impress on my peers the dreadfulness of the act perpetrated against me and how lucky I was not to have lost an eye. Much was made of the fact that had I not been bending down at the time, the stone might have hit me a little lower. What the headmaster did not know, and of course I did not tell him, was that I was bending down only to pick up an equally lethal stone to hurl at the boy who then threw one at me!

A tiny minority of bullying incidents, like child abuse referrals, will result in court action or other sanctions like exclusion. In extreme circumstances this may be the right thing to do. But most of the time in child protection we are talking about more routine interventions; about rebuilding relationships, not ending them; about how to help people to move on into better functioning rather than simply looking to hold certain individuals up for condemnation.

My worry is that, when it comes to bullying, we are often happy to deal with it at the level of punishment, but we rarely go on into more positive approaches which both create better relationships among those involved and establish prevention and protection for the future. In effect, this section aims to encourage schools to put bullying alongside other issues of child protection and to see what results. (I do not intend to cover the same ground as recent extensive publications on bullying, including the pack circulated by the DfE in 1994.)

Circular 10/95

There is some support for this dual approach in DfE/DfEE documents. The child protection circular 10/95 makes a passing reference to bullying and the importance of staff being ready and prepared to respond appropriately. Pupils should have confidence that they will be listened to, here as elsewhere. Most of the time, this should be enough to bring about the necessary response within the school. The draft of the circular said that where bullying persists so that a child is at risk of 'significant harm', 'both abuser and abused' should be referred according to local procedures.

There was no equivalent paragraph in the circular which this one replaced and the statement did not appear in the final version. I am not sure that the social services would know what to do with such a referral! As we have seen in Chapter 2, their definition of abuse tends to concentrate only on parents and carers. An allegation of physical bullying by a teacher might be within their remit; bullying by a child who is not a member of the family would probably cause them some problems.

However, the principle is sound. The inference is that the child who has been injured to a significant degree, may require help in order to 'promote their health and development'. The long-term effects, as well as the immediate medical concern are the focus here: ensuring that a child who has been through a bad experience is offered all possible help to prevent it becoming a major disturbance to their life. There might be a support group available, training in assertiveness or even self-defence, individual counselling, etc. Clearly the situation would have to be extraordinary to go to these lengths but the school has a role in ensuring that a proper assessment is made, though much will depend on local priorities and resources.

The needs of the bully may arouse less sympathy (though, of course, like me, the same child might appear in either category over time), but help for them is likely to be even more urgent. There is a growing awareness of abuse by children and young people, primarily within the family or when acting as carers. A child who has been responsible for a major incident at school, however, is likely to become something of a football in terms of agency responsibility.

A school could, quite rightly, see the bully as 'suffering or at risk of significant harm' and therefore as much in need of services as the victim. Continued behaviour of the same kind is likely to be a continued source of difficulty for both the child and the family. Not addressing the child's needs now will probably lead to greater problems in the future. Perhaps the bullying is an indicator of problems at home, a failure of parental care, etc. Perhaps the bully is, in turn, being abused by someone else. All this could make a substantial referral under the Children Act.

Circular 8/94

Social services are more likely to see bullying as an 'educational problem' unless the circumstances are very unusual, such as sexual abuse. And they may well be right. Take, for example, the guidance on bullying in circular 8/94 on 'Pupil Behaviour and Discipline', part of the *Pupils with Problems* set. Paragraphs 55 and 56 make clear the responsibility on the school to deal with such incidents, and to be seen to deal with them. Failure to act may be interpreted as condoning the behaviour and schools are expected to be aware of the issues and to plan accordingly:

> The Secretary of State recognizes the very real difficulties which often face headteachers, deputies and their staff in their daily dealings with pupils on matters involving behaviour and discipline. This Circular does not underestimate these difficulties. The Secretary of State also recognizes the very substantial good practice which already exists, often in schools with the greatest difficulties. The Circular reflects the success which many schools already achieve in fostering good behaviour among their pupils and aims to encourage the further spread of that good practice. It draws on the findings and recommendations of the Elton Committee and their implementation in schools. It encourages headteachers, in consultation with their governing bodies, staff and parents, to develop whole-school behaviour policies which will be clearly understood by pupils, parents and the school staff.
> (Paragraph 6)

A 'child-protecting school' will be aware of all this, and be continually engaged in doing it. Seeking to live up to such expectations clearly means ensuring that children treat each other with the same kind of respect and care as they are treated by the staff. Children may bring immense behavioural problems and anti-social attitudes to school with them; no teacher should be expected to carry the can for that. But a school committed to dealing with bullying will expect to be continually confronting such ideas and promoting a positive alternative which is actually acted out by staff and encouraged in pupils. Without it, bullying is inevitable and children will be put at greater risk of harm.

Circular 9/94

The circular on 'The Education of Children with Emotional and Behavioural Difficulties' is equally significant. It recognizes that poor behaviour may be an indicator of a special educational need which has not been properly addressed:

Some children's learning difficulties will have caused or aggravated their emotional and behavioural difficulties, often accompanied by a significant loss of self-esteem. Other children's emotional and behavioural difficulties may have given rise to their learning difficulties, by impeding access to the curriculum through, for example, the *aggression*, depression or hyperactivity they have displayed. Some children may be bright but frustrated or suffering from *serious emotional disturbance*. (Paragraph 4; my emphasis)

The same point is made in the *Special Needs Code of Practice*. Para 3.66 says that 'emotional and behavioural difficulties may become apparent in a wide variety of forms – including... *'disruptive, anti-social and unco-operative behaviour; frustration, anger and threat of or actual violence'*. Para 3.65 says that such behaviour may result *'from abuse* or *neglect'* and para 3.68.viii includes among the evidence that schools should collect in order to make an assessment, whether the child *'has participated in or has been subject to bullying at school; has been subject to neglect and/or abuse...'* (my emphasis throughout).

Bullies may be telling us that they have special educational needs. Their behaviour is the evidence of it. There is also a recognition of the significance of the home environment in defining SEN, of the need for schools to work closely *with* the parents of such children, not against them, if at all possible (paragraphs 26–30) and the importance of the pupil's perspective, including anything they may say about problems at home. While there can be no presumption that such children have been abused, paragraph 32 reminds staff to be alert to the possibility.

It is the clear intention of all this guidance that this process of assessment, understanding and response should be just as thorough for the pupil who is aggressive and even violent towards others as it should be for the child with a physical disability who might be the object of their bullying. Children are less likely to bully, or be violent towards teachers, if their educational needs are being met. That is a major challenge in the current financial climate, but entirely consistent with everything we have seen already about preventing abuse and protecting those at risk.

1994 Bullying Pack

This resource, based on the outcome of a DfE-funded research programme at Sheffield University, was made available to all schools in 1994. The take-up was high. There was also an accompanying video outlining various projects undertaken in Wolverhampton under the 'Safer Cities' initiative. A summary may be useful to indicate its scope:

- a whole-school policy on bullying;
- bullying, facts and figures;
- how much bullying is there in school?
- teaching strategies relevant to bullying;
- working with pupils involved in bullying situations;
- beyond the classroom;
- case studies;
- resource materials;
- The Sheffield Project;
- advice for pupils, parents and families;
- material for overhead transparencies.

Any school wanting to address this issue should be looking at this material. Many LEAs have been working on strategies to support its use and encourage the adoption of locally-devised anti-bullying policies. Like the circulars, it tends to emphasize the positive, preventative aspects of the issue, rather than dwelling on the punitive, disciplinary aspects. The sections on strategies for working with pupils and on looking at how the school might need changing in order to reduce the likelihood of bullying, are particularly informative.

Conclusion

The designated member of staff for child protection is not officially responsible for dealing with bullying as well, but I am increasingly convinced that the tasks are best done together. This will enable the possibility of abuse, in either bully or victim, to be recognized and the same philosophy applied in both areas of work. I end this Chapter where I ended Chapter 1 – with key principles arising from the Children Act 1989. The following should inform everything we do in all the areas I have covered:

- listening to children;
- working in partnership;
- identifying 'children in need';
- promoting the upbringing of children by their parents;
- providing supportive services;
- ensuring continued protection.

REFERENCES

Department for Education (1994) *Pupils with Problems*, collection of circulars including 8/94 and 9/94, HMSO, London

Department for Education and Employment (1995) *The Protection of Children from Abuse: The Role of the Education Service*, circular 10/95, HMSO, London

Department for Education/University of Sheffield/Calouste Gulbenkian Foundation (1994) *Bullying – Don't Suffer in Silence*, HMSO, London

Department of Health, (1991) *Working together under the Children Act 1989*, HMSO, London (op cit)

Johnson, B (1994) 'Teachers' role in the primary prevention of child abuse', *Child Abuse Review* vol 3, p 259–71

Lawlor, M (1993) 'Assessment of the likelihood of primary school teachers believing children's disclosures of sexual abuse', *Child Abuse Review* vol 2, p 174–84

NAHT (1993) *'Care and control of pupils/students'*, National Association of Headteachers Memorandum, NAHT, London

NSPCC (1994) *Protecting Children – A Guide for Teachers in Child Protection* NSPCC, London (booklet)

Olweus, D (1993) *Bullying at School: What we Know and What we Can Do*, Blackwell, Oxford

Sharp, S and Smith, P K, (eds) (1994) *Tackling Bullying in your School: A Practical Handbook for Teachers*, Routledge, London

Social Services Inspectorate/OFSTED (1995) *The Education of Children who are Looked After by Local Authorities*, Department of Health, London

Tattum, D P and Herbert, G (1993) *Countering Bullying: Initiatives by Schools and Local Authorities*, Trentham Books, Stoke-on-Trent

Webb, S (1994) *Troubled and Vulnerable Children: A Practical Guide for Heads*, Croner Publications Ltd, Kingston-upon-Thames

Whitney, B (1994) *The Children Act and Schools*, Kogan Page, London (op cit)

4

Protecting Children at Work

WHAT TEACHERS NEED TO KNOW

Background

In the Spring of 1995, a factory in Staffordshire assembling activity packs for a supermarket chain, was fined £16,500 for various offences arising from a raid by officials towards the end of 1994. Most of the fines related to serious breaches of Health and Safety regulations (faulty wiring, blocked fire doors, unguarded machinery, etc) but there was also a specimen charge of the illegal employment of children. An unknown number of children had worked there over the previous few months; after school, late into Friday evenings, Saturdays and Sundays.

The raid was captured on film and formed part of a Channel 4 documentary in which the adult in charge claimed that he was doing a public service in keeping the children off the streets in a warm and supervised environment. Many people would agree with him, at least until there was a fire or an accident. At court, a spokesman for the firm said that they had been unaware of laws relating to the employment of children and that countless other employers in the area also used children as workers. He was probably right. The illegal employment of children is commonplace, affecting an estimated 6,000 children in Staffordshire alone. Does it matter?

On first thought, issues around the protection of children in part-time employment might not seem very relevant to teachers. Surely they have enough responsibility, as we have seen, for children while they are at school and for monitoring their safety within their family, without also having to worry about what they are up to while trying to earn themselves a bit of pocket money? It is also fair to say that the statutory responsibility for monitoring child employment lies quite clearly with LEAs and not with schools.

However, there are two main reasons why some awareness of these issues at school level is essential if children are to be given the care and information which they need in order to ensure their protection:

There has traditionally been a link between problems of school attendance and part-time employment
This is why the historic duty to regulate it has always rested with LEAs rather than, for example, social services departments or the Health and Safety Executive as might be expected. This was originally based on the fear that children might be working when they should be at school. While this is still an issue for a few, especially in some areas and for older children, it is now more a case of making sure that children's participation in education is not adversely affected either by getting up too early or staying out too late at work. Does anyone check, for example, whether a poor attender also has a part-time job? Education should be a high priority in a child's life so schools should expect to take some interest in anything which might make that more difficult.

Schools are in the best position to raise these issues with children and parents on a day-to-day basis
Does anyone think to ask, if a child has a bad back, a fracture or some other injury causing them to be off school, whether it might have been sustained while working? This is certainly more common than we ever know under normal circumstances and questions might need to be asked *before* simply authorizing the absence. Schools also have a crucial part to play, as part of the PSE (Personal and Social Education) curriculum, in raising awareness of the existence of national regulations which control both the hours children can work and what they can do. Most parents and children are not aware of them; some are happy to disregard them until challenged. The legal duty lies with the employer, but teachers are in an ideal position to encourage responsible and sensible behaviour. Schools can circulate leaflets, organize assemblies, create opportunities for class discussion, etc.

School-leaving age

Teachers are also best placed to promote greater awareness of the age at which children may leave school and start work. There is considerable confusion about this, even among specialist agencies, job centres, etc. This chapter relates to the legal protection afforded to all children under the minimum leaving-age, *not just to those who are under 16.* Many parents, most employers and even some headteachers, think that children can leave school from their 16th birthday. This impression was, unfortunately, reinforced by the latest edition of the Parent's Charter (delivered to every home), which clearly states that parents have 'a duty to make sure your child goes to school until he or she is 16'. (p.9)

In fact, for children with birthdays early in the academic year, it may be six months *after* they are 16 before they can leave school, or work in school hours. The arrival of a National Insurance number also misleads many parents and children into thinking they can get a job any time from then on. However, *all unlicensed employment of children is illegal* before either the Easter holiday (for those with birthdays before January 31st), or the end of May (for all the others), of the academic year in which the young person becomes 16. (The single leaving-date expected with the Education Act 1993 has not yet been implemented.)

Why now?

It is particularly important that these issues are addressed now as 1996 should see new by-laws in every LEA area as a result of Directive 94/33 from the European Council. This requires all local authorities to update their laws by June 1996 in order to achieve general parity across Europe (though many will not have time to do so). Although the United Kingdom negotiated significant exemptions, which still leaves a rather different approach here than in most other EU countries, particularly for 16–18-year olds, this attempt at greater standardization for younger children is most welcome. The Employment of Children Act 1973, the last opportunity to ensure a consistent approach across the country, was never enacted and there has been considerable variation until recently, with few LEAs giving child employment much priority in their work.

This chapter gives a very brief summary of the history and some of the recent research and explains current law and practice in the light of the EC Directive. (Appendix 2 offers a resource which could be used in direct work with children, especially those in National Curriculum Year (NCY) 7/8.) Giving children the information they need to protect themselves is just as important in this context as all the work which is done about 'stranger danger', drugs, etc. Staff from the LEA's education welfare/social work service may be available to help with leaflets, local procedures, etc.

History

Many people assume that the exploitation of children at work disappeared with Dickens. As was seen in Chapter 1, children have not always been seen as in need of any special protection and this was nowhere more true than in the workplaces of 19th-century Britain. The industrial revolution led to a massive increase in the use of children as a cheap and numerous source of labour. This had always been true of more rural cottage industries, farms and smallholdings. This is familiar territory for our awareness of child employment:

> According to the historian E P Thompson, of 419,590 factory workers in the main branches of the textile industry in the early years of the 19th-century nearly half were under 18 years of age. Young children were paid somewhere between 2s and 3s (10–15 pence) for a 72-hour week. Dr. Turner Thackrah of Leeds wrote in 1832 of the children he watched leaving the Manchester cotton mills as 'almost universally ill-looking, small, sickly, barefoot and ill-clad. Many appeared to be no older than seven.' (Moorhead, 1987 p.7)

The state initially regarded employment as a more useful occupation for poor and abandoned children than education, though from 1802 regulations began to restrict their work at night and the age at which working life could begin. It appears that these rules were largely ignored however, not least because those responsible for enforcing them were themselves often the owners of the mills and factories concerned!

The 1833 Factory Act introduced external inspections; the Mines Acts outlawed the employment of children under 10, and then those under 13, but it was the introduction of more universal education and its element of compulsion which eventually led to serious inroads into the view of children as economic producers. By 1880, most children under 13 were expected to be in school at least some of the time, though practice was again inconsistent.

What may come as a surprise is that many of the laws which still operate towards the end of the 20th century date from over 70 years ago. Some are actually pre-1900. The Employment of Women, Young Persons and Children Act 1920, and the Children and Young Persons Act 1933, still form the basic legislative framework (see pp 90–91). Despite the renewed interest caused by the EC Directive, this illustrates how low a priority has been given to this issue by successive governments since the war, in contrast to all other areas of children's lives where there has been constant intervention to promote their welfare. As well as the non-implementation of the 1973 Act, an ideal opportunity was missed with the Children Act 1989.

Health and safety

Are children still at risk of death and injury as they were in the past? Of course there have been massive changes since the 19th century, but those with responsibility for the pastoral care of children should at least be sensitive to the fact that the issues have not entirely gone away. There are certainly a significant number of deaths every year as a result of accidents to children at work, most of whom would be working in places considered too dangerous for legal employment such as factories or other industrial undertakings. However, there is little national documentation and monitoring on which to draw.

Some injuries would be on farms where, ironically, the law is more relaxed for members of the proprietor's family (despite the obvious dangers). Others involve paper boys/girls being knocked off their bikes or mugged for the considerable amounts of money some are expected to carry. There appears to be a degree of tolerance in society in this area (no requirement for helmets and children being allowed to drive tractors on private property, for example), in contrast to all the procedures which would be invoked in the event of deaths and injuries caused by negligence and neglect within the family. Such prosecutions as there are often result in derisory fines with courts sometimes appearing to side with the employer in seeing LEA officers as interfering busybodies. This is in marked contrast to the USA where a major burger chain paid a US$500,000 settlement for breaking child labour laws.

Health and Safety legislation requires that an employer shows a duty of care towards the young people in their employment. They are the same as any other employee. Failure to protect them, deliberately seeking to exploit them or flouting legal requirements which employers have a responsibility to find out about, is a betrayal of trust. The effect on the child of a work-related accident is just as devastating as any other exposure to danger; it may have a dramatic effect on their education and development, even cause them long-term disability. Taking advantage of children, or giving little thought to the dangers which they may encounter, is to my mind every bit as abusive as many other kinds of behaviour which normally incur sanction and public disapproval.

Children's accounts
Research has revealed a catalogue of examples which make for pretty uncomfortable reading:

> I got my fingers stuck in the sole-cutter.
> When I was hemming a skirt the needle went into my finger.

I was making a kebab. When I put it in the hot oil it fell on my feet. It melted through my trainers and my feet went red hot, it went. Saw my bones, you could. It burnt through my skin.
I sliced half of my finger with a knife.
I cut my hands on a blade for cutting bacon and a knife went into my leg when I walked into it.
I was beaten up on my paper round and had my money stolen.
I was working on a machine and my hand got stuck. It nearly ripped my hand off.
I was on a milk float when the driver pulled the brakes. I fell out and broke my right leg. (Pond and Searle, 1991, p. 18/19)

A Low Pay Unit study in 1985 found that 30 per cent of working children had been injured at some time, but, as many of them were working illegally, few sought medical help. Of course such accidents might happen at home or in the street for other reasons, but it seems ironic that so little attention is paid to such risky activities. We do not allow children under 16 to buy cigarettes (though they can sell them or smoke them!), buy a lottery ticket or drink alcohol in pubs. We are, however, often indifferent to what they might be doing in factories, building sites or farms, or we might even think that it can do them no harm. Ignorance is far from bliss for the children concerned; like the 14-year old crushed to death by a cow and another who lost a leg under a tractor; the 15-year old who died after being overcome by fumes in a factory; the 12-year old killed selling flowers at the roadside or the 8-year old who died under the wheels of his father's lorry.

Definition of 'employment'

It is difficult to be precise about what work children do because of the problems of definition and the generally undercover nature of much of their employment. It is important to draw a distinction between jobs like errands, car-washing for neighbours, helping around the home, etc (not 'employment' within the meaning of the word) versus those jobs which come within the regulations. Employment is any work done for a commercial enterprise or in any business carried on for profit, *even if the child is not paid. All* such work should be licensed by the LEA; if not, the employer is committing an offence, *even if they are employing their own child.*

So, helping your dad wash the family car is not employment; going with him to the garage where he works and washing the cars on the forecourt is. Mucking out your own horse at the riding stables is not employment; cleaning out the owners' horses and supervising lessons is (even if you do not get paid for either task!). No child can legally do *any* work of this kind before the age of 13, except where *only* family members are employed in the business, in which case the minimum age is still 10 for certain kinds of employment (mainly light agricultural work).

Babysitting

The most obvious exclusion from these regulations is baby-sitting or being *'au pair'* for a family, which is not 'employment' as it is not done for a commercial enterprise. In effect, children are 'self-employed' in such work and so outside the regulations, as are all those who do paid work for individuals rather than businesses. There are actually no rules about the minimum age for undertaking such responsibilities, although the age of 13 also provides a sensible guideline for leaving a child in charge of other children.

Parents remain responsible for their children if they leave them in the care of an under-age sitter, but anyone may do so, provided they are not putting *either* child involved at unreasonable risk of harm. This also means that there is no control over the hours children may spend in babysitting, unlike the very strict controls when it comes to employment. It is difficult to see how there could be any kind of enforceable regulation in this area. Despite the obvious anomaly of this situation, as babysitting, in particular probably accounts for many of the tired children or empty desks the next morning, at least most such activity is relatively safe.

There is, however, growing awareness of babysitting as a context for abuse both by adults against children and by young people themselves against younger children. A further unregulated area of concern is the risks posed by unofficial car-cleaning at traffic lights in major cities where again there is no employer. This too is subject to no control (except as it may relate to unauthorized absences condoned by parents). Individuals who employ children to do odd jobs should not expect them to carry out adult tasks and some LEAs may still seek to licence them to give them some protection.

Legal employment

All legal work must be 'light duties' only and most children who work legally do paper rounds. Others work in shops and markets, deliver leaflets, pick seasonal fruit, do cleaning and waitressing or work with animals. A few children have more glamorous and high profile jobs such as modelling, filming and acting. These are normally, but not always, closely monitored, especially if any time off school is required. (Absence is not permitted for any work other than work experience and licensed performances – see below pp. 87–90.)

In general, we consider such jobs quite harmless, and a government minister pilloried the European Union at a party conference for
trying to restrict them further. But it might be considered that getting
up in time to start work at 7.00 am, while it is still dark and in all
weathers, on days when you still have over six hours at school to
follow, with perhaps another round in the evening before doing any
necessary homework, is more than enough for a child of 13 to manage.
That makes a 9 or 10-hour working day – more than I am expected to
do! Certainly our European partners see the whole idea of paper
rounds as bizarre and outdated and do not understand why we need
children to do it.

Illegal employment

The real problem is illegal employment about which, by definition,
we know little. *Any* employment of a school-aged child in a commercial enterprise is an offence by the employer unless they have obtained a licence for that child, even if the work is otherwise within the
regulations. Many of the infringements are minor, and it is difficult to
enforce some of the more archaic restrictions at times, especially those
relating to Sundays. Many adults, including teachers, feel some sympathy for children's efforts to help support themselves and admire
their initiative; many parents are far from cooperative when it comes
to ending illegal jobs. For some families, the money from children's
work is essential. Poverty can also lead to other problems such as
illegal childminding while parents have to work during school hours
or late at night.

Interestingly, Pond and Searle's research found that most child
workers were from more affluent families and were earning extra
money for themselves rather than children from poorer families
earning essential income to help their parents. The idea that children's
income is vital to the family economy appears to be true only for a
few. In general, children from these families lack the local opportunities available to their better-off peers and do not have access to
transport to work away from where they live. However, as there are
no longer any regulations about minimum (or maximum) wages, it is
perhaps these children from poorer families who are most likely to be
exploited or who will be most willing to put themselves at risk.

But this desire for financial independence can lead children into
unregulated and unsupervised workplaces, which is clearly not in
their best interests. No child of school age should be working in a pub
or factory, on a building site, in a chip shop, take-away or commercial
kitchen or be using various specified equipment. They should not be
lifting heavy objects, working with fuels, vehicles, chemicals or sol-

vents, sorting refuse or going up ladders to clean windows! Common sense tells us that some places are dangerous and children should not work there. No one really knows how many do so and few people take much notice of them when they do.

Pond and Searle found that 43 per cent of their large sample of Birmingham children between 11 and 16 were working (*excluding* babysitting etc), of whom 74 per cent were working illegally. They estimated that this would equate to 12,000 illegally employed children in the city, compared with the 4,000 who were licensed. Other research (Jolliffe et al, 1995), has found remarkably similar results. In this sample of 1,600 10–16-year olds in Greenwich, 41 per cent had jobs, of whom 78 per cent were working illegally. Children were walking dogs classified as dangerous, working on barges and, in one case, patrolling as a gamekeeper with a loaded shotgun and setting traps!

Hours of working

Employment can be illegal on three counts: working under 13, the type of work done and the hours worked. Children may not report for work before 7.00 am or remain after 7.00 pm on *any* day, (though paper boys/girls are often expected to do so). They may not work more than two hours on a school day; either two hours after school or one hour before and one hour after (so long as it is for the same employer). This is clearly intended to make sure that they give school work sufficient priority and attention. As will be seen later, the LEA has power to prohibit any employment for a given child if it takes the view that the job is detrimental to their education or health (provided they know about it).

These rules are routinely broken: in markets and seaside cafes, video stores, corner shops, supermarkets and football clubs using ball boys/girls for evening matches, let alone more clandestine activities. Children can work either five or eight hours on a Saturday, according to their age, with similar provision for school holidays, but the work must always be between 7.00 am and 7.00 pm. Sunday working has always been severely restricted to only two hours in the morning in most LEAs, with some by-laws allowing none at all. This is clearly an anachronism and may become more generous in future, but LEAs have no discretion in this area at present as it is in the core legislation.

Pond and Searle found examples of children working up to 22 hours a week in a clothing factory and a 15-year old working 46 hours a week in a hotel. Even in school holidays children can only work a weekly maximum of 25 hours (aged 13–14) or 35 hours (aged 15–16) and there must be proper breaks, with no more than 4 hours work at a stretch. (The EC Directive requires children to have a break from work at some point over the summer holiday.)

It is difficult to make a fuss when served by a young person in a late-night chip shop (when three regulations might be being broken at once). Perhaps, however, it is only through such public pressure that attitudes will change. Is it right that children should be doing work for which 'adult' charges are made? An example from my own experience is a tyre and exhaust centre whose employment of children only came to light after a customer complained about the work being done by a boy of 14 when he had been charged skilled mechanic's prices!

Pastoral responsibility

Awareness of all these issues will help the teacher, especially those involved in pastoral care, to be sensitive to what children might be doing at work. It is important to be clear that neither children nor parents are legally responsible; the onus is on employers. But school staff may want to discuss with parents whether their child's part-time job (which they may know very little about), may be having an adverse effect on their performance in school or is exposing them to unnecessary dangers. It seems that a few hours work may be beneficial, but working more than about 12 hours a week tends to be associated with poor educational performance.

Any evidence of bruising, injuries, cuts, accidents, etc which are said to have happened at work should be reported to the LEA so that they can be investigated further. There may be other children involved. Some parents cannot be relied upon to make sure that their children are safe, even late at night. Whether or not such incidents are seen as child abuse, and there are examples which I believe come very close to it, awareness of them is an essential part of child *protection* (see, for example, the UN Convention on p. 24).

Work experience

Children in the final year of compulsory education can be given opportunity to experience the world of work as part of their educational programme. This is not 'employment' and so does not come within the scope of the regulations directly. Children may be able to do things as work experience which they cannot do as a job outside school hours, provided it is safe, though placements must conform to other legislation such as the Factory and Licensing Acts. This can cause some confusion for children, employers and parents, but the context for such activity is intended to be quite different from employment. Work experience is education – an extension of school – unpaid, in school time and monitored by school staff.

Schools carry significant responsibilities for work experience, including the health and safety aspects. Employers cannot simply make their own arrangements; doing so would constitute 'employment'. It is expected that placements are appropriate to children's educational needs and that they provide genuine learning opportunities. Guidance from the Department for Education (DfE 1995) outlines the various roles both within and beyond the school:

Senior management
A school's commitment to work experience should be shown in the School Development Plan, with a clear and coherent structure within which the placements are provided. One member of the senior management team, or a steering group, perhaps involving expertise from outside the school, should oversee the arrangements.

Designated coordinator
It is best if one person is responsible to whom other staff, parents, employers and children can relate directly. It is their responsibility to monitor and evaluate the placements. There should be a strategic policy to which they work which ensures that placements are not being used inappropriately or putting children at risk.

Professional support
Schools should make use of the expertise provided by their LEA, Careers Service, Training and Enterprise Council, local businesses, etc. It may be appropriate to use school governors in the local community or invite business representatives to sit on the steering group.

Parents
Parents should be kept fully informed and given details of placements in advance which indicate the learning benefits which should result and the nature of the tasks involved. It must be made clear that children are *not* being given permission to go to work.

Work experience should be explored through the curriculum both beforehand and through follow-up. The content should be evaluated and the learning objectives assessed. This provides a safeguard against those situations which are simply looking to use young people as cheap labour and those which have not paid sufficient regard to their safety. There are no precise regulations about the length of placements. In the past, the DfEE has considered that more than two weeks is exceptional, though there are circumstances where extended arrangements, or even a regular number of days each week might be appropriate for those close to the leaving age. This is likely to become more commonplace in the light of the closer relationship between education and training at government level.

Children should not participate in work experience outside school hours unless the particular job requires it. Pupils should be seen as still within the school's care while on placement and so not expected to do anything which exposes them to unnecessary risk. The DfEE recommends that any employer used must have a clear health and safety policy (a requirement for those with over five employees), and that staff should satisfy themselves about the arrangements by personal visits. While on placement, pupils should be accepted by the employer as in need of appropriate supervision and support.

Work experience placements have to be shown as 'authorized absence' under the Education (Pupils' Attendance Records) Regulations 1991. Children who do not turn up when required should, however, be marked 'unauthorised absent'. (For further details see the Education (Work Experience) Act 1973 and the accompanying regulations summarized in the DfEE booklet.)

Children in entertainment

Finally in this section, some information about children of school age who take part in entertainments (which now includes modelling, advertising, cultural events and professional sports activities in the light of the EC Directive, as well as shows, cabarets, TV, films, theatres, etc). Most organizations which operate in this area are familiar with the requirement for such activities to be licensed by the LEA under the Children and Young Persons Acts 1933/1963 and the Children (Performances) Regulations 1968. There is also specific legislation designed to protect young children from 'dangerous performances' such as circuses.

These regulations relate to:

- performances for which a charge is made (but specifically excluding events put on by schools);
- any professional performance on licensed premises (eg, a club);
- any broadcast performance;
- any recorded performance.

The LEA has to be satisfied about fitness and health and there must be a 'matron' or chaperon present, usually a parent. Places of performance may be inspected as regards dressing room facilities, toilets, etc and there are various regulations relating to hours of work, breaks, etc. While some of these rules date back to a time when theatres were considered rather dangerous places for impressionable young minds, the recognition of some of the risks inherent in child modelling/photography are particularly welcome.

There has been some concern that such activities could easily be misused by those who have an interest in creating opportunities for child sexual abuse and this has been a major loophole in legislation until very recently. It was always said that children who walked about while modelling were in an 'entertainment', and so eligible for a licence, whereas those who stayed still were working! This meant that all catalogues showing clothes for children under 13 were the product of illegal employment, which was consequently, generally unregulated. Any suggestion that children are involved in 'posing' or 'photographic modelling' should be followed up if there is any concern that it might not be bona fide. The new expectations provide rather more safeguards, though whether LEAs will have sufficient resources to carry them out is another question entirely.

The significance of this issue for schools relates both to the need for reasonable vigilance and also to awareness of the implications for attendance and absence. All such activities must be properly licensed *before* children are given permission to be absent from school for either rehearsals or performances. Agencies, film companies, etc are required to give sufficient notice for licences to be issued in advance, though live TV shows often have to be dealt with at the last minute.

Requests for absence without prior approval from the LEA should *not* be authorized under normal circumstances. Parents who request leave of absence for shows, etc should be asked if licences are needed first. Headteachers are free to raise objections if the amount of time missed is proving a problem or if the child is engaging in unlicensed work. Absences beyond a few days for older children usually justify setting work to be done while away from school. (Special regulations apply to schools specifically designed for drama/music/film students.)

LEA POWERS AND DUTIES

The legal framework

This section is intended as a quick reference guide to the law for teachers. It may help in answering questions from parents, pupils and colleagues and in understanding the responsibilities carried out by education welfare officers on behalf of the LEA. 'Child' in all these provisions means a child of compulsory school age.

There are two key Acts of Parliament:

Employment of Women, Young Persons and Children Act 1920
This relates to employment in industrial undertakings and includes a general prohibition against children being employed in factories or

industrial 'outwork' at home. In general, it is policed by Health and Safety officers.

Children and Young Persons Act 1933 (as amended by the Children and Young Persons Act 1963 and the Children Act 1972)
This is still the core legislation within which LEAs have to operate. It contains two significant sections:

1.   s.18(1) says that no child shall be employed:

   (a)   so long as s\he is under the age of thirteen years, or
   (b)   before the close of school hours on any day on which s\he is required to attend school, or
   (c)   before seven o'clock in the morning or after seven o'clock in the evening on any day, or
   (d)   for more than two hours on any day on which s\he is required to attend school, or
   (e)   for more than two hours on any Sunday (This may be changed by a future Deregulation Act, but a whole weekend limit is most unlikely.)
   (f)   to lift, carry or move anything so heavy as to be likely to cause injury to her\him.

2.   s.18(2) gives local authorities the power to make by-laws which may further define arrangements for authorizing, licensing or prohibiting employment (but without the power to make any of the core requirements in s.18(1) more generous).

Other Acts of Parliament which may be relevant include:

Agricultural (Health, Safety and Welfare Provisions) Act 1956 (amended by the Health and Safety at Work Act 1974)
This includes restrictions on the operation of machinery and other safety requirements for under 18s.

Factories Act 1961
Various requirements relating to machinery, safety, etc (mostly amended by the 1974 Act).

Licensing Act 1964
This prohibits the employment of any person under 18 on licensed premises (though some LEAs allow children to be employed as a waiter/waitress provided they do not serve alcohol, and children may be licensed to perform an entertainment). By-laws often include a prohibition on children selling alcohol unless it is in sealed containers, so they might be allowed to work in an off-licence.

Employment Act 1989
This generally eased restrictions for older young people but contains important regulations about street trading. There are also other more obscure laws, still in force in part, such as the Pedlars Act 1871, the Pawnbrokers Act 1872, the Dangerous Machines (Training of Young Persons) Order 1954 and the Betting, Gaming and Lotteries Act 1963 which prohibits employment of under 18s in betting shops etc (though over 16s may sell lottery tickets).

Registration procedures

Any child of school age who is employed in a commercial undertaking or in a trade or occupation carried on for profit, must be licensed by the LEA, even if they are employed by their parents in the family business or work unpaid. It is the responsibility of the *employer* to complete the necessary procedures. This normally involves:

- the completion of a form applying for a licence for each child employed who is under school-leaving age (this form may also include a requirement for parental consent);
- assessment by the LEA of whether the job, the hours worked, the age of the child, etc, fall within the regulations, and whether there is any evidence that employment may have a detrimental effect on their education;
- a medical check, either by the Health Authority, or, increasingly, by a questionnaire filled in by the parent;
- the issuing of a licence (sometimes on a temporary basis in the first instance), which should be kept by the employer (or carried by the child in some LEAs).

The main incentive for employers to go through this process is that those whose child employees are licensed are far more likely to be covered by the firm's insurance company in the event of an accident theft or injury. Unlicensed children will often not be recognized as employees and therefore will have no claim against the employer's liability insurance. Their parents would also be able to take civil action against the employer personally for damages to obtain compensation

In addition, registration gives legal protection against possible prosecution and entitles employers to expect responsibility from the child concerned. I have known a case of an unlicensed paperboy who kept the payments he had collected door-to-door (in itself a very risky activity which is illegal under some by-laws). The employer had no right to claim the money as the boy was not legally his employee so there was no proof that the money belonged to him!

Enforcement

Even if the employment is legal in terms of age, hours, etc, it is illegal unless this procedure has been followed. Most LEAs should operate a system of six-monthly or annual reviews in which local employers are required to complete a return indicating all the children in their employment. This enables children in work to be identified. Failure to complete such a return when requested is an offence in itself.

EWOs may also do 'spot checks' or early morning visits to verify that children are working within the law. Gross abuses may result in prosecutions, though these are rare, not because children are not working illegally, but because few LEAs resource the work sufficiently and prosecution is difficult with such ancient laws. Most LEAs rely on information from parents, teachers and members of the public to inform them of children who are working so that checks can be made as they are reported.

LEA officers have no automatic right of entry to premises where they suspect that unlicensed children may be working. Normally persuasion is sufficient. In extreme circumstances, s.28 Children and Young Persons Act 1933 allows for a magistrate to make an order which enables entry to search for children, but these are very rare. However, no force can be used. The Police have greater powers, not least under s.46 Children Act 1989 which enables them, by force if necessary, to remove any child judged to be 'suffering or at risk of significant harm'. If factory premises are involved, it is likely to be easier for action to be taken by Health and Safety Officers using the 1920 Act.

Infringements of by-laws rarely become the subject of legal action; they are simply far too common, though the power to warn persistently negligent employers is useful. Two powers under the Education Act 1944 may be used more frequently:

- An LEA can, by written notice served on the employer, prohibit the employment of a particular child, or otherwise restrict it, 'where he/she is being employed in such a manner as to be prejudicial to (his) health or otherwise renders (him) unfit to obtain full benefit from the education provided for (him).' (s.59(1)) This requires the LEA to know of an actual child being illegally employed; it cannot be used as a blanket prohibition. Ignoring this notice is an offence. If a child's work is interfering with school attendance, this action (or just the threat of it) can be particularly helpful in negotiating a greater commitment from the child. Teachers should be aware of this possibility and ask the LEA to make use of it where relevant.

- An LEA can, by written notice served on any parent or employer require them to give such information to the LEA as may be necessary in order for them to ascertain whether a child is being employed. (s.59(2)) Again, ignoring this notice is an offence (the only legal obligation on parents in relation to employment).

Children outside the maintained system

There has been some confusion in recent years over the fact that the legislation has not been amended to take account of the growth in new kinds of schools or children educated 'otherwise than at school'. The powers in the Education Act 1944 relate only to 'pupils registered at a county school, voluntary school or special school'. This therefore leaves out those children in the independent sector, in grant-maintained schools, city technology colleges and pupil referral units as well as all those being educated by their parents or attending FE colleges. These children's employers are still subject to the same requirement to register their employment, but enforcement against them and especially the prohibition of particular individuals is much more difficult.

There is also uncertainty about the position of permanently excluded pupils who are being educated through home tuition and not on a school roll. The 1933 Act speaks only of days when children are 'required to attend school'. It could be argued that these children could work more than the specified two hours a day, for example, even in term-time, as long as they are available for their tuition when required (perhaps only two or three hours a week). These issues have been the subject of lobbying with the DfEE for some time and are still far from clear.

REFERENCES

Department for Education and Employment (1995) *Work Experience: A Guide for Schools*, HMSO, London

Jolliffe, F et al (1995) *Child Employment in Greenwich*, Borough of Greenwich, London

Moorhead, C (1987) *School Age Workers in Britain Today*, Anti-Slavery Society, London

Pond, C and Searle, A (1991) *The Hidden Army: Children at Work in the 1990s*, Low Pay Unit, London

Searle, A (1993) *Child Employment/Children in Entertainment*, Training Advisory Group Booklet, National Association of Social Workers in Education/ Association of Chief Education Social Workers, London

5

Allegations Against Teachers and Other Staff

Setting the priorities

The main text of this book ends where it began with the issue of allegations of abuse by teachers. This layout is deliberate. While teachers' needs are important, the primary focus has to be on children and the role of schools in ensuring their protection. One of my aims in writing is to redress what sometimes seems to be an imbalance in perceptions in the education service. Getting protection right for the adults must be subsidiary to getting it right for the children, though I would also argue that there is rarely a fundamental conflict between the two.

The anxiety in this area is understandable but misplaced. Good practice in caring for children and identifying abuse goes on unnoticed all over the country every day; most teachers are seen as caring and supportive by children and their parents. The headlines focus only on two things: the genuine tragedies which may result from false accusations and the even greater disaster of those cases proven to be true. I make no apology for beginning this chapter with a reminder that some concerns are justified; abuse by teachers can, and does, happen. Such situations have to be properly acknowledged within interagency procedures for dealing with professional abuse, *before* we jump on too quickly to what should be done about the rest.

Two horror stories

R L was a male primary school teacher in a South Wales authority. In March 1994 he was convicted of eight counts of gross indecency against six boys at his school aged between 9 and 11 and sentenced to seven years imprisonment. He had been at the school since 1976, never arousing any suspicion, but had been abusing children for ten years. What began with complaints from a parent about physical punishment turned into a major enquiry involving sexual abuse with all the classic elements of touching and 'grooming'.

Over 100 children may have been involved over the years but, as no records were kept and earlier concerns were not referred on for investigation, only a small number could be proven. There was, said the social services assistant director 'a lack of preparedness (within the school) to take seriously, and follow up, children's statements and believe the unbelievable'. (*Community Care*, 1994)

J D was a male student nursery nurse at a college in the north of England. In April 1993 he was convicted of nine offences of indecent assault against children and also sentenced to seven years. The offences occurred during his placement at two LEA nursery schools, over several months, during the course of the school day, in the classroom. In all 60 children were interviewed. There were 45 confirmed disclosures of abuse, including both boys and girls, involving vaginal and anal digital penetration as well as less invasive touching and stroking.

These offences took place during what were seen as quite innocent actions such as lifting children up, sitting next to them, under a table, etc and not in more potentially risky situations such as taking children to the toilet. No one was aware at the time of what was going on, even though other staff were present in the same room at all times. Although J D had not received a good report from the first school where he was on placement, he was popular and well-liked in the second and well-accepted by the children and the staff.

The Hunt Report

The Hunt Committee, which looked into the case of J D and reported in September 1994, was generally critical of the school's awareness of child protection issues and of the way in which the LEA handled the case once it became public. It found many failings in common with those in the case of R L. Staff had not received adequate training, especially about sexual abuse; they did not follow the correct procedures; a teacher went too far in investigating the concerns herself (almost ruining the whole investigation when J D managed to plant the idea that the abuser being referred to was another child with the same first name as himself). There was general disbelief that such a thing might be possible. Children were not listened to; the existence of one case was not seen as an indication that there might be others;

and warning signs such as excessive rough and tumble play were not recognized.

A key issue raised by this second case is a reminder that not all adults who have access to children at school are teachers. This is not, of course, to say that classroom helpers, students, playground supervisors, volunteer parents, meals staff, etc pose a greater threat than anyone else, but vetting procedures will operate more formally for teachers than for others. However, it is important to remember that *every* adult who works with children should act appropriately. DfE guidance (before the case of J D) suggested that only those with 'substantial unsupervised' access to children should receive a full police check. In my opinion this is not sufficient to cover all reasonable risks and policies must certainly involve everybody.

A review of procedures for recruitment, supervision, training, etc may be especially relevant here, especially where adults come into the school community for a short time or when staff turnover is high. Given even the possibility of abuse by older students, for example, on work experience or, as in this case, on placement, all staff should be made aware of the need for reasonable vigilance and care. (ACPCs and LEAs should be addressing this issue in response to circular 10/95, but see also DfE circular 9/93.)

Abused children/abusing teachers

The Hunt report focuses both on how the abuse could have been prevented or detected earlier and on how the school/LEA responded to the complaints once raised. Procedures for each were equally flawed. For me, this is vital in understanding what happened. Is it coincidence that there should actually have been such an incident in a school which was clearly so ill-prepared? Was it just chance that these schools provided an opportunity for a determined and skilful abuser when the staff were also under-trained and apparently so unaware of the statutory procedures? I do not think so. There is a clear connection.

These cases, and others like them, form a bridge between the protection of children and the question of abuse by teachers. Dealing with *both* issues is part of the evidence of a 'child-protecting school'. Ultimately, getting the whole package right is in everyone's interests. Schools which are thorough about the protection of children will, I believe, also offer teachers effective protection against malicious or unreasonable allegations *and* be able to identify those cases which do give rise to genuine concern.

Such examples are very rare, though not unique. They should remind us of the importance of being open to the possibility that such things can, and do, happen in schools; that teachers and other staff can, and do, abuse children. Denial that children could ever possibly be at risk in *this* school, or that any teacher we know could ever pose such a threat, would both be equally misguided. This issue is not an optional extra within procedures for responding to child abuse, it is an integral part of them. All professionals must expect to fall in line with prescribed guidelines. LEAs, governors and senior staff are failing in their 'duty of care' if they do not see their significance.

Recognizing the risks

Facing up to the reality of abuse by teachers and others is partly about addressing the unique nature of the teacher/pupil relationship, in which young children in particular invest a great deal of meaning and commitment. It is also about acknowledging that few other adults outside a child's family spend so much time with them in situations where there is such potential for disaster. While the dangers should not be overstated (perhaps many teachers will never have looked at themselves in this light and will find the following paragraphs rather shocking), there needs to be a clear recognition of the risks. I would identify three in particular:

Power
Teachers carry a great deal of power over children's lives; power has a tendency to corrupt. If it is abused, it can act as a potent force for continued secrecy, just as it does with a parent. Penelope Leach, in her book *Children First* talks about children's involvement with adults as an unremitting experience of power (Leach, 1994). It may not always feel like this, but the teacher/pupil relationship is far from equal. Schools are hierarchical institutions with a clear pecking order, in which children are at the bottom. Education law gives them no status at all as decision-makers. They are not even 'customers'; that privilege is reserved for parents. Children are merely recipients; society expects them to do what teachers say.

Abuse always involves the use of power; it requires a dominant partner able to exercise control over the other. The more teachers seek to operate in partnership with children, rather than hoping to impose their will on them, the less likelihood there is of attracting individuals into the profession who are interested in exploiting young people and see schools as an easy place to do it. Such thinking is often seen as rather 'trendy', even subversive. In fact, it is essential if teachers want to change the climate away from one which puts them directly in the line of fire.

This is why, of course, we must never revert to using physical punishments in schools. Not only because it will provide an opportunity to the adult who actually enjoys inflicting pain on children, as has certainly happened at times in the past, but because it is entirely the wrong kind of relationship between teacher and pupil. It would reinforce the model based on power, when what we want are positive examples of partnership from which children (and their parents if necessary) can learn. Seeking new kinds of authority-based approaches will simply set teachers up for more scandal; either for the few who will go over the top or for the many more who will have to defend their actions and risk censure in a climate which is far from clear about what the rules are. Not being allowed to hit children at all is a major protection for *teachers*, let alone the pupils.

Sexuality

Few would dispute that the 'caring professions' are at greater risk than others of getting over-involved with children and young people. Working with children fulfils emotional needs in us; that's why we do it. No wonder it sometimes goes horribly wrong. If you have never met a paedophile, do not imagine that they are all cruel inhuman monsters or pathetic individuals who could never hold down a responsible job like teaching. Many would claim to love children and to be good at working with them; people maintain their position and status for years without anyone suspecting. Often the evidence is not all one way.

An essential element in training for those who work directly with sexually abused children and adults is recognizing their own sexual feelings and how they relate to the job. This can be very embarrassing but is immensely valuable. There is often uncertainty in our own sexual experience and attitudes; 'grey areas' which need to be acknowledged. Teachers rarely have an opportunity to go through this process and are, as a result, much more vulnerable.

It would also be foolish to ignore the significance of older pupils experimenting with their sexuality, and therefore open to exploitation by those who they see as role models. Schoolboy/schoolgirl 'crushes' have not entirely disappeared even in today's more cynical times; young teenagers emerging into adolescence carry a particular attraction for many adults (not only men). Why else is there continuing use of the schoolgirl as an image in soft-porn magazines or the promotion of the ever younger-looking 'waif' as the ideal supermodel? Even the concept of 'toy-boy' has its implications. There is great ambivalence in our society which reflects, at least in part, a powerful folklore about the sexuality of the young which can put teachers in a very ambiguous role. I wonder how many false allegations have been the result of spurned attraction or misinterpreted friendship?

Conflict

Then there are the obvious issues of discipline in which teachers are required to act in ways which may make children angry or which challenge their understanding of themselves. It is no surprise (or it shouldn't be), that this whole situation is sometimes the opportunity for abuse, or carries obvious potential for false allegations. Clearly there is much more likelihood of physical violence against a child who continually frustrates and disobeys you. Many abusing parents are stuck in this spiral.

Children may seek revenge against those who they feel have wronged them at school or even use violence themselves. Teachers cannot always be expected to meet their expectations or do what they want; some children will know no other way of resolving conflict and will seek constantly to provoke. Even the most long-suffering and experienced professional may sometimes snap under such pressure.

Responsible employers must face up to all this and not put staff in impossible positions. Such an attitude is fair to neither children nor teachers. This is why the issue is included in this book, and why it has featured more prominently in recent government circulars than used to be the case. There are real risks to be addressed. Simply ignoring them, hoping they will go away or seeing things only as the responsibility of the children, is as much a failure to act responsibly as failing to carry out local procedures when required.

'Working Together'

As has already been noted, the interagency child protection guide includes the following statement within its section relating to education: 'For all educational establishments, the procedures should cover circumstances where a member of staff is accused or suspected of abuse' (para.4.36). There is also related guidance in paragraphs 5.20.4ff which deals with residential establishments, including schools:

> In order for abuse by staff to be prevented or readily discovered, it is essential that children and staff are encouraged to report their concerns to the appropriate persons in the local area. The procedure for doing this should be included in the responsible authority's or school's written guidance, and the message reinforced wherever possible through training and supervision. Both children and junior staff will require reassurance about the importance of their making such reports. Those in authority should equally be encouraged to treat all such concerns raised with them by children and junior staff speedily and appropriately, and to ensure that correct and effective action is taken. The procedures should also make clear the action that should be taken if the member of staff feels that inappropriate or insufficient action has been taken.

Where abuse by a member of staff is suspected, the action to be taken would be the same as with any other suspected abuse, ie, the local SSD or investigating agency should be informed immediately, and other agencies involved as appropriate. In such circumstances the need for the fullest possible cooperation with those investigating the allegations is of great importance, and those with responsibility for the... school should ensure this is provided wherever possible.

It must also be recognized that there may be abuse by staff in a residential setting which pervades the whole staffing fabric with the involvement and collusion of several, possibly senior, members of staff. Where such abuse is suspected, it will be necessary for the police and senior staff from the SSD, when agreeing their strategy for investigation, to pay regard to the need for secrecy, even if this means a delay before action is taken. This will need to be weighed carefully against the rights of the individual children concerned to protection from the suspected abuse.

I believe that this guidance identifies issues which are relevant for *all* schools, not only those which are residential where, admittedly, there may be a particular need for more thoroughgoing procedures (see, eg, Kahan, 1994). Cases of abuse at residential schools have been a major area of concern in the past because of the rather 'closed' nature of many such establishments caring, in some cases, for vulnerable children and young people away from the normal counter-balances of family and community. There is, at times, something of a conspiracy of silence in which even caring professionals can be caught up, where children who were a constant source of difficulty while at home or in a local school, are at risk of being quietly forgotten once they are out of sight.

Not all of the safeguards for such children promoted by the Children Act 1989 have been preserved in recent years, especially those relating to smaller schools, no longer subject to inspection as 'children's homes' as was the Act's original intention (s.292 Education Act 1993). Residential schools should still take careful account of the guidance in Volume 5 of the Children Act series where relevant, though all the signs are that, under pressure of deregulation and a desire to avoid unwanted outside interference, inspections will probably be less frequent and less rigorous in future (until the next scandal that is!)

Principles

Some of the more generally applicable points arising from *Working Together* are:

Children have a right to make complaints.
This is often seen as a relatively radical idea, though I do not really see why. The UN Convention on the Rights of the Child, ratified by the United Kingdom in 1991, gives children a right to freedom of expression and to have their views respected. The Children Act says much the same. The novelty of the idea is rather greater in education than elsewhere. I do not believe that telling children that they have access to genuinely independent processes for resolving disputes will open the floodgates of unwarranted accusations. This has not happened in other establishments such as children's homes which have introduced formal procedures. Indeed, I would argue that the absence of agreed complaints procedures makes it *more* likely that trivial issues will be escalated into child protection enquiries because there is no accepted alternative in which children or parents may have confidence. The Hunt report proposes an LEA-based 'ombudsman' for such situations but few have responded. (see below p. 107 for a possible model of a complaints procedure.)

Children are entitled to be listened to.
This is not the same as saying that they should always be believed. But, given that opportunity for complaint is available to them (and many schools send at least unconscious signals that complaints by parents or children will receive pretty short shrift), what they say should then be taken seriously, not immediately dismissed as untrue. It is futile to argue either that children must always be believed or always not believed. Neither position is realistic. Some incredibly unbelievable stories turn out to be true; some which seem entirely plausible are a total fabrication. Only proper investigation will resolve the issue. The first step is to make it clear that the child will be heard – openness, opportunity, empathy, etc.

There should be clear, written policy for dealing with such issues.
This is surely best for everyone, including any teacher who is the subject of an allegation. Policies should set out the rights of *all* the people involved, not just the rights of the child. They should contain provision for the resolution of disagreements, timetables for decision-making, appropriate procedures for ensuring confidentiality and clear indications of who is responsible for what. Policy should be widely discussed, not just imposed and, if possible, shared in advance of it being needed, so that there can be no accusation of making it up as we go along. (See, eg, Cheshire County Council (1995) for an excellent example.)

Criteria for decision-making should be open and consistent.
There is a genuine fear among teachers of decisions being taken behind their backs in smoke-filled rooms, without them being made aware of what is going on. Parents are entitled to information when they are the subject of an inquiry. There is no reason for professional staff to be treated any differently. There should be scope for challenging decisions, a right of appeal and to know what the evidence is. Some of the most tragic cases involving ruined reputations have shown little regard for these principles.

Colleagues should act responsibly.
It can be very awkward when a junior member of staff feels that a more senior colleague has acted inappropriately or has major grounds for concern. Abuse of power in this context can lead to a closing of ranks which could be highly dangerous. Staff are entitled to feel that acting in the best interests of children will not be seen by their managers or by their colleagues as underhand. Equally, no one should seek to sustain a personal vendetta, against either a child or a teacher, by abusing their professional status. Where complaints are against very senior members of staff, even perhaps the designated teacher, all adults in the school community should feel that the chairman of the governors or the LEA is available to them.

Teacher training and supervision should recognize child protection issues.
I have seen little evidence that this happens in initial training so it must be a crucial part of INSET. This issue has to be something which is regularly talked about. All staff should have access to someone who is responsible for their personal and professional development. (This can often be less true of teachers than of other professions.) No one should be left alone to 'do their own thing'. Such a 'hands-off' approach is courting disaster and is an abdication of managerial responsibility. Staff should expect to be confronted by questions like 'did you feel you handled that child properly?', 'how might you have dealt with that situation better?', in both groupwork and personal assessments, without feeling unduly threatened or defensive.

Allegations of abuse by teachers must be investigated within the defined interagency procedures.
This point is explored below. Cooperation is a legal requirement in all child protection work; there is no place for 'special cases' which, in effect, invent new criteria for a given individual.

These points essentially place the protection of children alongside proper procedures to promote the best interests of teachers, *except where the two are in conflict*. Each party is entitled to proper protection, but there can be no question of seeing the interests of the teacher as paramount; priority must always be with the child. Erring on the side of caution, to the extent that children at genuine risk have no opportunity to call attention to their plight, is not an acceptable way of minimizing any possible risk of false accusation.

There will always be tension: both children and teachers *may* seek to exploit any possible weaknesses in the procedures. As would also be true if a child chose to make an accusation against me, all of us while entitled to be treated fairly, probably have to accept that our needs are secondary. We are the adults in the situation. If we cannot live with that, then perhaps we should not be working with impressionable, confused, sometimes hostile children and young people. It is in the nature of childhood to act irresponsibly from time to time. We sometimes expect too much of children; put too much of the responsibility onto them. That is not to say, however, that nothing can be done to minimize the risk to either party and to anticipate the possibility of children acting unreasonably.

DfEE guidance

The Department for Education and Employment expects that schools will have both effective procedures for protecting children *and* an awareness of what to do if a teacher is accused. In 1995 the Secretary of State made amendments to the Education (Teachers) Regulations 1993 at the same time as issuing circular 10/95 which was examined in more detail in Chapter 3. Together these set out a new structure within which LEAs, teacher organizations and ACPCs may work together to ensure good practice. This had previously been an area of some dispute with Directors of Social Services feeling that too much autonomy was being given to headteachers, and teachers' representatives feeling that there were not enough checks in the system to ensure that careers and reputations were not ruined without justification.

It is too early to say whether these varied expectations can all be met. The DfEE is clear that the welfare of children comes first. It is not the only consideration but it has to be the paramount one. The circular on Teacher Misconduct (11/95) has also tightened up procedures for banning the employment of those with any history of sexual offences against children, and clarified the grounds on which an individual may be barred (or unbarred) in the light of convictions, etc. This will all be helpful, though, in general, it is not the major area of difficulty provided governors make appropriate checks before appointment (eg, not employing anyone on 'List 99' which is held by the DfEE).

Dealing with allegations

The government has accepted that automatically suspending teachers subject to an accusation is not always appropriate. I have read of examples where teachers were suspended even though they, or the child, were not in the building on the day the alleged incident took place. This should not be necessary on such flimsy evidence. Even though suspension is, in law, a neutral act implying no guilt, in practice everyone appreciates that this is rarely seen to be the case. It should not happen in the face of all common sense or if there is no indication of continuing risk to this child or to any others by the teacher remaining at work.

However, it must also be recognized that almost as many allegations are found to have *some* substance as those which are dismissed entirely on investigation. A survey carried out by the DfE in 1994 amongst LEAs and reported in the draft of circular 10/95 (though not in the final version), found that 46 per cent of cases had some basis in fact, even though, as with all child protection referrals, only a tiny number actually resulted in prosecutions and convictions. The number of cases reaching court is not a fair measure on its own.

Where an accusation is made, the expectation now is that suspension should only happen when it is necessary. A claim of sexual abuse is clearly in a different category from disputes over the way a child was handled during an argument, for example. There is, as with all child protection referrals, some time for considered reflection about whether there is sufficient evidence to conclude that the child is at risk and what should be done about it. There is space to share this process confidentially with others. The headteacher and the governors will need to take account of:

- the seriousness of the allegation;
- an assessment of its plausibility;
- the risk of harm to the pupil concerned or other pupils;
- the possibility of evidence being tampered with;
- the interests of the school;
- the interests of the individual teacher.

They should do this in *full consultation with other key agencies and according to locally agreed ACPC procedures*, not on their own. It should not appear that there is a different set of procedures just for headteachers to use or that teachers are somehow above the system. All professionals who work with children should expect to be subject to the same expectations. There may be little choice, or decisions may be taken out of the headteacher's hands by a parent, but not all investigations lead to censure. People make mistakes; apologies and disciplinary procedures may be sufficient, even after a minor incident is proven.

More detailed advice (not as binding as guidance), specifically about teachers, is also now available and was attached by the DfEE as an annex to circular 10/95 (CLEA 1995). This also stresses that an allegation against a teacher should have the welfare of the child as the central concern as part of standard child protection procedures; children should be respected for what they say and an assessment made of what evidence there is to support any allegation before any action is taken. This advice should be widely discussed as part of the process of establishing appropriate local procedures. It has been a key part of the training for designated teachers for which I have been responsible.

General complaints

It is important to distinguish between child protection issues and other complaints of unprofessional conduct which should be dealt with differently. Children or parents may go to the SSD or to the LEA because they are not aware of an alternative when their complaint is actually not about child abuse at all. Headteachers, with support from LEA officers and advice from other agencies, need to make a decision about whether a complaint to them is a disciplinary issue alone, or whether it also raises specific questions of child protection. Not all abuse (eg, racist abuse) would normally require child abuse procedures. Figure 5.1 is a possible model for making such a decision, involving some kind of panel, including representation from *outside the school*, which could be convened at very short notice.

Most teachers would, I am sure, say that they simply wish to receive the same degree of 'innocence till proven guilty' as should be accorded to anyone who is the subject of any allegation. It may be reassuring to discover the range of obligations now placed on professionals to ensure that the rights of parents are not overlooked, even if they are suspected of abuse. The principles of natural justice should apply no less in a school.

This seems entirely fair, even allowing for the sense that the potential betrayal of a professional, trusted relationship, means that there is inevitably some difference, as there would also be for a social worker, EWO, priest, doctor or youth worker in the same position. Interviews away from school premises and at a reasonable time of day; rights to representation and speedy decisions about whether or not an allegation has any basis, would also seem to be axiomatic, as would informing people of outcomes and offering staff care/counselling as part of the package during the process.

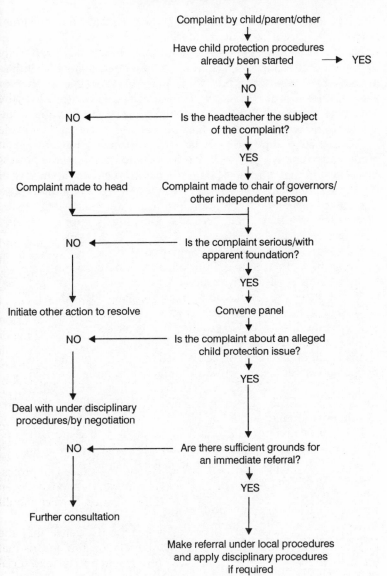

Figure 5.1 *Complaints procedure*

Touching children

I have lost count of how often I have heard or read that the Children Act prevents teachers from touching or restraining children. I have no idea where this notion has come from; probably only from the guidance issued to local authority residential care staff by the Department of Health about how they should handle children in a crisis. It is not in the Children Act itself. Of course the climate has changed; children are more likely to resist authority than in the past and, like adults, they are more able to seek redress, even through the courts, if they feel they have been wronged. But touching children is not always abuse and the Act in no way supports such a notion.

Circular 10/95 affirms the teacher's right to touch children, both in emergencies and when they are distressed and need comfort. No one has ever said that teachers should not cuddle a child who has fallen over, hold their hand, or comfort them when sad. Particularly with younger pupils (though common sense again suggests that things are different with older young people), touching is appropriate and affirming.

However, the circular also recognizes that innocent actions can be misconstrued; children may find some touching uncomfortable and invasive and, occasionally, touching has been used for less than innocent purposes. Adults can be inappropriate in their behaviour; I have seen teachers make unwarranted remarks or cause children embarrassment by physical contact. Particular care should be exercised where children have special educational needs.

Inadvertent touching can be avoided by sensible precautions. Any deliberate attempt to use physical contact to intimidate, humiliate or threaten a child is wholly unacceptable. We must appreciate where the boundaries are. A young person's objections to any touching should not automatically be dismissed or, worse still, treated as some kind of misbehaviour. They may, for example, not wish to attend a school medical or receive immunization; they may refuse to shower or undress in public. No one should make them do so.

Any disciplinary confrontation which is escalating into possible physical force by a teacher should be de-escalated again as quickly as possible, if necessary by withdrawing from the situation, even if it means loss of face in the short term. Any use of physical restraint to prevent injury or damage within the school must be recorded in writing and monitored. If an incident occurs, it is common courtesy (and practical common sense), that parents should be informed by the school *before* they hear the story from the child, or they may fear a conspiracy where none exists.

In an emergency, the minimum force necessary can be used to prevent a child from injuring themselves or others. Circular 9/94 on the Education of Children with Emotional and Behavioural Difficulties, in the *Pupils with Problems* pack (DfE, 1994) gives advice on this specific issue (See also NAHT (1993) op cit). A child may have to be touched in an intimate place to help them over a piece of PE apparatus or to prevent a fall. But contact must remain, at all times, entirely professional. It is sometimes possible to ask for the child's consent if they need lifting or carrying for example, and to make it clear that *the child* is in control of how much they want to be touched. Their sensitivities should be respected, especially those which arise from any religious or cultural traditions which are not shared by the teacher.

But there is no reason why children who are 'punching the living daylights out of each other' should just be left to get on with it, even if this does pose some risk to those intervening, and even if a complaint from a parent might result. (They might also complain about the fact that no one intervened!) Some training and preparation for such a possibility might be reasonable rather than simply walking into it. This area is difficult and you may be open to accusations of unreasonableness, whatever you do. Witnesses are always useful, written records should be kept and advice and support should always be available.

Most importantly of all, teachers should not lose their temper with children, however much they may appear to deserve it! Children should *never* be seen as 'deserving' abuse; either physical, emotional, verbal or racist. Bullying by any adult is unacceptable. Touching must never be to meet the teacher's needs, only ever to meet the child's needs. A climate within the school which fosters mutual respect and regards aggression from anyone as unacceptable will help to protect both teachers and pupils from straying over the limits.

Taking children away overnight

The role of *in loco parentis* is very important when children are away from home in the care of teachers, especially when trips involve overnight stays. (Be careful, incidentally, that consent forms are signed by parents with 'parental responsibility' wherever possible (see Whitney (1994) op cit). Such situations raise additional questions about appropriate behaviour and the need to make sure that staff act responsibly. Common sense suggests that teachers should take proper measures to protect both themselves and the children from any possible misunderstandings or unacceptable behaviour in this context, when relationships may be more relaxed or opportunities presented which are out of the ordinary.

The school mentioned in the introduction to this book might have been wise to have staff check the children's dormitories in pairs; perhaps two women for the girls and a man and a woman for the boys. Try to have another adult present in any situation which might be open to compromise; for example, if ever an item of clothing has to be removed (eg, after an accident) or if children need help with toiletting. Remember that the need for privacy among adolescents, in particular, is essential.

It is *not* true that since the Children Act teachers cannot give medication, put on a plaster or help a child with their inhaler as any parent would do if they were there at the time. Sometimes this idea is used only as an excuse. If someone with parental responsibility has given written consent for you to do this (and it is best, if the child has particular needs, to ask the parent to say in advance on the consent form *exactly* what they want you to do), this could not possibly be seen as an assault.

The teacher in this position is no different from a foster-carer or step-parent; if anything, their role is *clearer* since the Children Act. They have 'care of the child' and when in that role, *where they have prior consent from someone entitled to give it*, they may do everything that is reasonable to carry out that other person's parental responsibility on their behalf and to safeguard and promote the child's welfare. (This situation is specifically envisaged by the Children Act ss.2(9) and 3(5) which cover the position of people who do not have parental responsibility for the children for whom they are caring.)

An exception again might be where the child objects, especially older children and young people. Acting against their will may not be appropriate, unless it is a matter of life and death or you have clear grounds for knowing that you are carrying out the parents' wishes. I do not think any teacher could be criticized for having to restrain a young person who is drinking too much on a school trip for example, even if they protested about the need to do so at the time. What must be clear, however, is that excessive force was not used or that the opportunity was not abused in some way while the young person was intoxicated. As before, professional conduct throughout, a balance of sexes among the leaders and more than one adult present whenever possible would be sensible precautions, as is keeping a written record of any incident which may be questioned later.

Conclusion

Teachers are entitled to know that they have a clearly thought out policy behind them to cover all these issues; not one which requires them simply to make their own mind up at the time and thus take sole responsibility for any mistakes. There should be codes of conduct in place; guidelines should be agreed and monitored, principles should be written into behaviour policies, brochures and statements of equal opportunities. Clearly men are at particular risk and they should be thinking through the issues, but there is no need to become paranoid.

There will always be the danger that a child will exploit the professional's personal vulnerability, either physically or by making up false allegations. All those who work with children have to accept this possibility. We must have reasonable expectations of each other. (I was once asked by a teacher colleague why I was refusing to go into a teenage girl's bedroom and force her out of bed!) Staff can help one another by being prepared to work in pairs or to act as witnesses in sensitive situations. We must avoid the obvious dangers and ambiguous opportunities without being over-precious. We must be vigilant about any actions by colleagues which are unacceptable, without fear of being thought intrusive.

When children do accuse unreasonably, or when they pose a direct physical threat, disciplinary issues must be balanced with a longer-term pastoral perspective. Blaming the child, insisting on their removal from the school, industrial action, etc are understandable reactions but are generally unhelpful. The CLEA guidance makes no mention of exclusion or other punishments as an appropriate response to such a situation and calls for 'appropriate counselling and support' which takes into account the child's needs.

Damaged children in particular do not always act in reasonable ways; they are, after all, children and may have had bad experiences with adults in the past which have made them suspicious and even malicious. But schools with proper policies, which support and care for *both* their staff *and* their pupils by trying to build relationships based on equality and mutual respect, should be able to manage the vast majority of situations to everyone's satisfaction. The two tasks are not in conflict – quite the reverse.

Schools which consciously set out to protect children also have far less reason to fear those same children feeling the need to make up stories against teachers or to blow trivial incidents up out of all proportion. Schools which do not see the need to plan for all these responsibilities suggest, at least to me, that their children are more likely to feel hostile and alienated. Such schools are also far more at risk of becoming a refuge for that extremely rare individual who does pose a genuine threat and so are more likely to become the subject of a scandal or to lose good teachers unnecessarily. Any of these possibilities would seem too high a price to pay for not trying to get it right.

REFERENCES

Cheshire County Council (1995) *Code of Conduct for Teachers*, Education Services Group, Cheshire

Community Care (1994) 'Teacher's Secret', *Community Care*, 16–22 June 1994, 1021, p. 14

Council of Local Educational Authorities (1995) *Teachers Facing an Allegation of Physical/Sexual Abuse: Guidelines on Practice and Procedure*, Circular 95/12, CLEA, London

Department for Education (1993) *Protection of Children: Disclosure of Criminal Background of Those with Access to Children*, Circular 9/93, HMSO, London

Department for Education (1994) *Pupils with Problems*, collection of Circulars, HMSO, London (op cit)

Department for Education and Employment (1995) *Misconduct of Teachers and Workers with Children and Young Persons*, Circular 11/95, HMSO, London

Department for Education and Employment (1995) *The Protection of Children from Abuse: The Role of the Education Service*, Circular 10/95, HMSO, London (op cit)

Department of Health (1991) *Working Together under the Children Act 1989*, HMSO, London (op cit)

Kahan, B (1994) *Growing up in Groups*, National Institute for Social Work, London

Leach, P (1994) *Children First*, Penguin Books, London

NAHT (1993) *Care and Control of Pupils/Students* (op cit)

Newcastle upon Tyne City Council (1994) *Independent Enquiry into Multiple Abuse in Nursery Classes* (The Hunt Report), Newcastle

Whitney B (1994) *The Children Act and Schools* (op cit)

Appendix 1: A Model Child Protection Policy

Circular 10/95 requires all educational establishments to develop a child protection policy *and make it known to parents*. This is a very helpful way of preparing the ground for any necessary referrals and provides evidence of competence. Such a policy might stand alone or be integrated with other related policies on bullying, special needs, behaviour, equal opportunities, sex education or pastoral care. It might be circulated to parents as a separate document or be included in brochures, handbooks, etc. A comprehensive policy will contain:

- a statement of the school's statutory obligations;
- an awareness of procedural responsibilities;
- a commitment of resources;
- expressions of openness towards children;
- curriculum issues;
- staff issues;
- complaints procedures.

Example policy

This school recognizes its legal duty to work with other agencies in protecting children from harm and responding to abuse. If staff have significant concerns about any child which *may* indicate physical abuse, emotional abuse, sexual abuse or neglect, they are *required* to discuss them with the agencies responsible for investigation and child protection. The designated teacher for child protection matters is...

Staff who have concerns about apparent injuries or who are told anything significant by a child, *must* report their concerns to the designated teacher. School staff do not carry out investigations, nor decide whether children have been abused. That is a matter for the specialist agencies. All staff should be familiar with the procedures for keeping a written record of any incidents and with the requirements of the local Area Child Protection Committee. Advice may be sought from the Local Education Authority, the Social Services Department or the police if staff are unsure how to proceed.

Child protection is important and the governors will ensure that sufficient resources are made available to enable the necessary tasks to be carried out properly. Staff will be released from normal duties for essential meetings, to prepare written reports or to attend training as required.

This school adopts an open and accepting attitude towards children as part of its responsibility for pastoral care. Staff hope that children and parents will feel free to talk about any concerns and will see school as a safe place when there are difficulties. Children's worries and fears will be taken seriously if they seek help from a member of staff. However, staff cannot guarantee confidentiality if concerns are such that referral must be made to the appropriate agencies.

Child protection issues will be addressed through the curriculum as appropriate, especially in Personal, Social and Health Education. The school will also ensure that bullying is identified and dealt with so that any harm caused by other pupils can be minimized. All children will be encouraged to show respect for others and to take responsibility for protecting themselves. Parents are expected to help children to behave in non-violent and non-abusive ways, towards both staff and other pupils.

Parents can feel confident that careful procedures are in place to ensure that all staff appointed are suitable to work with children. More informal procedures are also applied to voluntary helpers, non-teaching staff, etc. If it is necessary to use restraint against any child, or any child is injured accidentally, parents will be informed immediately. Children may not be punished within school by any form of hitting, slapping or shaking or other degrading treatment.

Any complaints about staff behaviour may be made to the headteacher, or to the chairperson of the governors. *All* those involved will be entitled to a fair hearing, both children and staff. Complaints which raise child protection issues will be reported by the school under local interagency procedures. The nominated officer for child protection within the Local Education Authority, if parents are not satisfied with the school's response, is...

Appendix 2: Training Ideas

INTRODUCTION

All Area Child Protection Committees should have a training group of some kind at which the needs of teachers can be addressed. LEAs have a duty in *Working Together* to ensure that designated teachers are trained and supported and should offer a range of training courses, either themselves or, preferably, in partnership with the ACPC. Staff whose regular work involves child protection should see such opportunities as a priority and their managers should ensure that they make use of them. *Messages from Research* (DoH, 1995, op cit) identified this as an urgent issue for teachers.

Some schools organize their own training, with support from outside, as part of the staff development programme. A particularly useful resource in planning such events is the booklet by Wonnacott (1995), which contains both guides to available training packages and a helpful grid setting out the various needs at different levels of involvement. All training should take account of the core areas identified here:

- awareness and recognition;
- policy and procedure;
- responding to children;
- responding to parents;
- impact on staff;
- child protection and the curriculum.

The ideas given below are not sufficient to plan entire courses. There is no replacement for interagency work at a local level in order to build good practice. What follows are some fragments from my own training experiences; outlines which could be incorporated into a course, or form the basis of discussion on less structured occasions. They may be sufficient to encourage the reader to participate in a planning group designing training opportunities for teachers and governors, or they may stimulate thought among colleagues on some of the issues. These particular courses are delivered by Specialist Education Welfare Officers in partnership with representatives from other agencies. There are also some ideas about working directly with children on both child protection and child employment.

A two-day programme

This is a programme used for ACPC interagency training in Mid-Staffordshire, under the leadership of accredited trainer/practitioners. Not all designated school staff are able to spare this amount of time, but this is the ideal as teachers can then train alongside colleagues from other agencies with whom they will be working. The course concentrates on understanding each other's roles in the child protection process and reflecting on one's own reactions to the issues.

Day 1
- 9.30   *Introduction*
           aims and objectives;
           recognition of personal and professional experience;
           sensitivity to different roles;
           groundrules – punctuality
                        – confidentiality
                        – respect for different views
                        – anti-discriminatory practice;
           domestic arrangements;
           space/privacy for individuals if required;
           introduction – name, agency, role, etc.
- 10.00   *Role-sharing and trust-building*
           experiential exercise about what we do;
           what we value about it;
           what we find difficult;
           identifying our own and others' skills, etc.
- 11.00   Break
- 11.15   *Categories of abuse*
           Presentation on definitions, statistics, etc.
- 12.00   *Acceptable/unacceptable behaviours*
           Experiential exercise about how participants feel about particular behaviours and whether or not they give any cause for concern – raises awareness of cultural and personal variations.

- 1.00 Break
- 2.00 *Managing our concerns*
  Input regarding personal and professional reactions.
- 2.15 *Case studies*
  Group exercises on a range of types of abuse which illustrate interagency working.
- 3.15 Break
- 3.30 *Feedback and review of the day*
- 4.00 Close

Day 2

- 9.30 *Introduction/reminders of Day 1*
- 9.35 *The statutory framework*
  Presentation on the Children Act, etc.
- 10.00 *Investigation under ACPC procedures*
  Joint SSD/police presentation on the referral and investigative process.
- 11.15 Break
- 11.30 *Case-conference exercise*
  Building on one of the case studies from Day 1 and looking at the decision-making process through a structured/narrated role play.
- 1.00 Break
- 2.00 *Care plans and core group*
  Group exercise arising from the case conference exercise and looking at key agency roles.
- 3.00 Break
- 3.15 *Unwinding exercise*
- 3.30 *The way forward* (individually and in pairs):
  what the course has meant to me;
  evaluation;
  further training needs.
- 4.00 Close

A one-day programme

The one-day programme contains selections from the two-day course, concentrating on the basics, with less time for experiential work through group exercises, etc.

A half-day programme

This course is specifically intended for designated school staff and is run as a half-day event (at limited cost to the school). The primary focus is on the role of the designated teacher and ensuring competence in their critical tasks. This course would be run in conjunction with the distribution of key literature including a handbook for the designated teacher and individual leaflets for all members of the teaching and non-teaching staff.

Programme

Session 1:   *The Children Act*
- Key principles;
- Statutory framework.

Core documents
- *Working Together;*
- DfEE circulars;
- ACPC/LEA handbooks and procedures.

Session 2:   *The role of the designated teacher*
- raising awareness;
- recognizing abuse;
- good practice in referrals, etc;
- interagency liaison.

Group exercise/case study;
Allegations against teachers/professional abuse;
Further training opportunities.

A short programme/INSET session

These briefing sessions are available to whole staff or smaller groups on a 'buy in' basis either at the end of the school day or as part of an INSET day. They are designed simply to familiarize staff with the existence of child protection as an issue; ensure that they are aware of the role of the designated member of staff; outline the basic framework of the law and introduce the information leaflets and procedural documents which tell them what to do. It often helps to address concerns about allegations against staff in this context.

Training for governors

School managers are essential links in the child protection chain, but few have much awareness of the issues. This is a course outline which is offered through the Staffordshire programme of support and training to governing bodies. It is delivered both as 'buy in' training for whole governing bodies on request (or groups of schools in an area) and as a 'one-off' event for interested representatives at modest cost. (It is, incidentally, vital that governing bodies are resourced to buy training now that it is included within the overall 'school effectiveness' budget heading rather than given to them separately.)

Also included below are two case-studies which have proved very effective as discussion starters.

Programme

Session 1: *Child protection: What governors need to know*
- Categories of abuse/identification;
- OFSTED requirements;
- DfEE circulars;
- Bullying Pack 1994;
- The Children Act 1989.

Session 2: *ACPC procedures*
- *Working Together*;
- Local ACPC handbook;
- LEA procedures handbook;
- Dealing with allegations against teachers.

Session 3: *Managing Child Protection*
- Case studies for discussion;
- Feedback;
- What happens next?/school policy issues.

Case studies

After reading the story, discuss the following:
1. What went wrong and why?
2. What should the governors do about it now?
3. What policy issues are raised?

Marie

Marie's mother has complained to the parent governor about the headteacher's response to an allegation of bullying. She says that Marie came home from school last week with two bruises to her face and a pain in her ribs, saying that she had been hit and kicked by another pupil at lunchtime. She had not said anything to anyone at school about it. On discussing it with the headteacher the next day, Marie's mother claims that the head said that this could not possibly have happened at school as the staff did not allow bullying; it was not a problem at this school. She also claims that the headteacher inferred that the bruises might have been caused at home. This has made Marie's mother very angry and she now wants the governors to deal with the matter or she will go to the press.

Carl

The Social Services Department have written to the LEA about an alleged failure by your school to follow agreed child protection procedures. Carl was found in the street late one night in obvious distress, claiming that he had been 'hurt' by his mother's boyfriend. On examination, there were signs of attempted buggery and other bruising and tears to his anus, going back over several months. At the case conference, which no one from the school was able to attend, a written report from the headteacher was tabled. This admitted that the class teacher had found Carl crying at school six weeks ago complaining that his step-dad 'hurts' him. She maintains that she reported this to the headteacher, though there is no record of the conversation. However, no further action was taken at the time. The head is very embarrassed about the whole situation. The class teacher is now on leave due to stress.

Child protection and the curriculum

Child protection issues clearly belong within the school's curriculum for personal and social/health education and the resources which are available focus on:

- exploring attitudes and values;
- developing personal and social skills;
- helping children to understand their bodies;
- building self-esteem;
- developing self-confidence.

Children, especially in Key Stages 2 and 3, need information about the existence of child abuse and the statutory network of services which are available (perhaps alongside other 'dangerous' behaviours like substance misuse). All programmes require flexibility to take account of individual circumstances and of the fact that children will be at very different stages in their level of awareness and experience. Delivery must be by people who are committed to the task and know what they are doing, if necessary by involving professionals from outside the school's usual teaching staff such as school nurses or social workers.

Teaching on these issues needs to be done in context, both as part of a relationship between this subject and the rest of the curriculum and as an expression of a partnership between the school, families and the local community. There must be a whole- school approach which reinforces what is done in the classroom and which involves all the adults in the school. Children need to see that there is a consistent commitment and that child protection is an identifiable part of the school's ethos. This will also encourage reluctant parents.

There are several published packs and programmes, details of which should be available locally. *The Listening School* (Gilmore and Dymond, 1993), is an excellent resource for addressing issues around sexual abuse with primary-aged children; a copy has been made available to all schools in Staffordshire. I have also used The Advisory Council on Alcohol and Drug Education (TACADE) material, *Skills for the Primary School Child*, which may now be a little dated (1990). Other resources are published by Kidscape, The Children's Society, Child-watch, Healthwise Ltd, the NSPCC and others. Addresses for these organizations and details of up-to-date publications should be available through your LEA Teacher/Advisor for PSE (see also the DfE (1994) Bullying Pack).

Where such events lead to children making disclosures, I particularly like the c-a-r-i-n-g principle in the TACADE material (with a warning about not taking the 'investigation' bit too far):

- creating a warm, supportive atmosphere;
- allowing children to express strong feelings;
- reflecting back and responding appropriately;
- investigating the situation with sensitivity;
- negotiating a way forward with the child;
- going forward, learning from mistakes, planning carefully.

Awareness of this framework shows that we are prepared for the possibility that what we are going to talk about may be very personal to the child. There are always dangers in this; they may copy what they have heard or invent a personal story because this is what they think you want them to do. But it may help the child to feel safe and so, either to take action to make themselves safer elsewhere or to make use of the opportunity presented at school, knowing that the teacher will know what to do. The teacher's own needs, if this material raises personal memories, must also, of course, be addressed by colleagues and managers.

Classroom resources on child employment

This is an idea which could be used with children to raise awareness of child employment issues and help them to protect themselves. The best time to do this is during Year 7 or early in Year 8. It will need to be supplemented by local information, leaflets, registration forms etc as required which should be available from your LEA/Education Welfare Service.

Child employment quiz

After a presentation on the issues, or as a way of opening up the discussion, this may help to reinforce the learning points (answers below!):

1. Beth wants to do a paper round. How old must she be?
2. Jasminda has been asked to babysit for a neighbour. Does she need an employment licence?
3. Steven has been told to come in at 6.30 am to bag up the papers for his round. Is this legal?
4. Anna has got a job in a shop on Saturdays. She is 14. How many hours can she work?
5. Leroy is helping in his dad's video shop after school until 7.00 pm Is this legal?
6. Lucy keeps coming into school late after her morning paper round. Can Education Welfare stop her doing the job?
7. Sanjay is sweeping up in a factory on Saturdays. Is this legal?
8. Joanne helps out at a hairdressers in school holidays. She is 15. How many hours each day can she work?
9. What is the minimum wage for children?
10. Who is breaking the law if a young person works without an employment licence?

Answers

1. 13 (14 in a few LEAs).
2. No, but children (and parents) should be warned about entrusting small children to their care for very long. If anything goes wrong, the parents of the baby are still responsible. Children under 13 should not be left in sole charge except in an emergency.
3. No. If the employer insists on it, get your parents to complain or try to find a job with a more responsible employer.
4. Five hours. There should be a one-hour break at some point.
5. Yes, provided his father has a licence from the LEA and Leroy works no more than two hours per day. (However, at least one LEA has banned all work in video shops on the grounds that children may be exposed to films which are suitable only for over-18s.)
6. Yes. If school/Education Welfare think that work is interfering with school, they can tell the employer to stop employing you. It is against the law to ignore this instruction.
7. No. Factories are dangerous places even when they are not in operation. No one can work there until they have reached school-leaving age. (Any work experience for older children must be very carefully supervised.)
8. Eight hours. Again with a one-hour break.
9. No limit! Beware of employers who are exploiting you. In what other ways might they treat you unfairly? Work is still 'employment'

if it is helping in a business, even if the child is paid nothing at all or is paid only in kind.
10. The employer. Children cannot break the law, BUT, they are the key to safeguarding their own protection.

REFERENCES

The Anti-bullying Game (1995) a therapeutic board game for children, Jessica Kingsley Publishers, London

Brown, D (1993) *Responding to Child Abuse*, Community Education Development Centre/Bedford Square Press, London

Charles, M and Stevenson, O (1990) *Multidisciplinary is Different* (op cit)

Gilmore, J and Dymond, P (1993) *The Listening School* (2 vols), Links Educational Publications, Pontesbury

Kidscape (n.d.) *Feeling Happy, Feeling Safe* and *Good Sense Defence*, Kidscape, London

MacDonald, S (1991) *All Equal under the Act?* Race Equality Unit, Leeds

Moon, A (1992) 'Child protection programmes in schools', *Journal for Pastoral Care and Personal and Social Education* 10, 1

Owen, H and Pritchard, J (1993) *Good Practice in Child Protection – A Manual for Professionals*, Jessica Kingsley Publishers, London

Wonnacott, J (1995) *Protecting Children in School: A Handbook for Developing Child Protection Training*, National Children's Bureau, London

Appendix 3: Glossary of Child Protection Terms

These are practical explanations designed to make it clear for the non-specialist what common words, phrases and acronyms used in child protection actually mean. They are not necessarily strictly literal or legal definitions but are an attempt to interpret the current jargon. There is a particular emphasis on the new terms which have arisen as a result of the Children Act 1989 which will still be very unfamiliar to many teachers but are commonplace among social workers. This glossary is intended in particular as a useful resource for case conferences! Words in bold print are defined elsewhere.

Abuse   Injury, neglect, or **harm**, either physical, emotional or sexual which is caused to a child by their **parent**/carer, either by deliberate acts or by failure to protect them.

Accommodation   The term now used to describe the service offered by the **local authority** when it looks after children on a voluntary basis (s.20 Children Act 1989). The status of such children is entirely different from those on a **care order** through the courts. All the **parental responsibility** remains with the **parents** and they may remove the child at any time without notice. Accommodation may be with a **foster carer** or a residential unit. (The word may also be used in connection with helping an alleged abuser to leave the family home.)

Action plan   An outline of the action which is intended once a court order is made so that the court can be satisfied that the **no order principle** has been met and that making the order is in the child's best interests.

Actual bodily harm (ABH)   Any hurt or injury calculated to interfere with the **health** or comfort of the victim, that is, bruising, minor wounds, etc. ('Wounds' must break the skin.) The injuries are less serious than with **grievous bodily harm**.

Adoption   The permanent assumption of **parental responsibility** for a child. This is the ONLY legal process which ends the actual **parents'** legal relationship with their child. There are now some examples of 'open adoption' in which some **contact** with family members is maintained, especially for older children.

Anal dilation   Opening of the anal sphincter muscles. Seen as evidence of sexual **abuse** in the Cleveland cases but rather discredited since the Butler-Sloss report questioned its reliability.

Anatomical dolls   Dolls with genitals and orifices which are used to help children explain what has happened to them. Not all professionals are agreed about their value.

Anti-discriminatory practice   An integral feature of social work which ensures that services are delivered in a way which respects differences of race, gender, physical and intellectual ability, sexual orientation, etc. Sometimes called anti-oppressive practice.

Area Child Protection Committee (ACPC)   The statutory body in each **local authority** (or smaller area), responsible for bringing key agency representatives together for the planning, monitoring and implementing of child protection procedures in their area.

Area Review Committee   A sub-committee of an **ACPC** which reviews procedures and/or individual cases and promotes good practice between agencies at the local level.

Assault   Usually linked with 'occasioning **actual bodily harm**' before it is considered an offence. A slap or push; any use or attempted use of physical force against another person. There are certain key exceptions including 'lawful correction' or 'reasonable chastisement' by a **parent** and in self-defence.

Attention Deficit Disorder (ADD)   The emerging term for children who are hyperactive or who have difficulties with concentration, both at school and at home.

Authorized person   A person who is authorized by the Secretary of State to bring care or supervision proceedings under s.31 Children Act 1989, in addition to officers of the **local authority**. Currently this covers only officers of the **National Society for the Prevention of Cruelty to Children**.

Buggery   Intercourse via the anus; an offence against any person under 18. Proof requires only the slightest degree of penetration. There is a related offence of assault with intent where there is no actual penetration.

Care Centre A county court which has full jurisdiction in all **public law** and **private law** applications, usually hearing those cases which are more complicated than usual. Most **public law** applications are heard at Magistrates Court level in the **Family Proceedings Court**, at least to begin with.

Care management The process by which an individual's needs are assessed, together with the planning and delivery of services to meet those needs. In some areas, the term 'care manager' has now begun to replace 'social worker'.

Care order An order under s.31(1) Children Act 1989 which places a child in the care of the local authority on the grounds of **'significant harm'**. The effect of a care order, which can be made on an interim basis, is to give **parental responsibility** to the **local authority** in addition to anyone else who has it, with power to restrict the exercise of it by others.

Centile charts A system of measuring children's weight, height, etc in a way which compares them with other children of similar age. Scores consistently below the norm may be an indicator of neglect or other **abuse**.

Child Assessment Order (CAO) An order under s.43 Children Act 1989 which requires any person with care of the child to produce them for an assessment, usually medical. The order lasts for a maximum of seven days and may specify that the child be kept in hospital overnight. There is no change in **parental responsibility**.

Child in need A child defined by s.17(10) Children Act 1989 as entitled to the provision of services to promote their **health** and **development**.

Child Protection Case Conference An interagency forum for gathering information about a child, making an assessment of current risk and planning what action is required to ensure their continued protection, including the possibility of admission to the **Child Protection Register**.

Child Protection Coordinator The term often used to refer to the **designated member of staff** in every school who is responsible for child protection matters.

Child Protection Investigation Team (CPIT) A team of specialist social workers from within the **social services department** responsible for making an initial assessment in response to a child abuse referral. They will work closely with the police and are responsible for making a preliminary decision about whether further action is required.

Child Protection Plan The agreed plan of action arising from a **Child Protection Case Conference** and carried out by the **key worker** and the **core group**.

Child Protection Register A central record, held on computer, of all those children in the area of an **Area Child Protection Committee** who have been defined as at risk of **abuse**.

Civil courts/proceedings Legal proceedings which are not criminal, that is, divorce, **care orders**, other applications under the Children Act 1989, etc.

Criminal Justice Act, 1988 (amended by the 1991 Act)   Made substantial changes to the way in which children's evidence may be used by the courts in criminal proceedings, including offences against the child, in particular the use of pre-recorded video evidence.

Comprehensive assessment   Assessment by a social worker of what services or court orders a child may require, involving the acquisition of a wide range of information, often according to a standard checklist, in order to provide a sound basis for future decisions. Such assessments should, where relevant, include information relating to the child's educational needs.

Conduct disorder   Behaviour in children which is anti-social and harmful to self or others, beyond the bounds of naughtiness. Such children may have been abused, have emotional and behavioural difficulties or be seen as beyond parental control/deviant.

Contact   The replacement for 'access' under previous legislation and broader in intention. Contact is any arrangement by which a child is enabled to see, visit, telephone or write to, or be contacted by, a **parent**, sibling, relative or other person, especially in the context of a dispute. Contact is usually related to divorce and separation, but is also a feature of arrangements made under a **care order** and some **adoptions**.

Contact order   An order under s.8/12 Children Act 1989 which requires the person with whom a child is living to allow them to have contact with another person, as defined by the order. They are intended to define the child's right to contact rather than the emphasis being on the other person's right to have contact with them. (No order means that all reasonable contact is permitted.)

Core group   A small interagency group responsible to the **Child Protection Case Conference** for carrying out in practice the agreed **Child Protection Plan**. It will always involve a social worker as **key worker**.

Court Welfare Officer   An officer, usually from the probation service (**Civil Courts** Welfare), appointed by the court to investigate the child's circumstances in **family proceedings**.

Criminal injuries compensation for children (CIC)   Children who have been the subject of violence may be entitled to financial compensation. Where a child is on a **care order** this may be an issue addressed by the **social services department** on their behalf.

Custodian of the register   A senior officer from within the **social services department**, responsible for the **child protection register**.

Designated member of staff   The term used by the interagency guide, *Working Together*, for a senior member of staff in each school, who is responsible for ensuring good practice in child protection. Many LEAs call them **child protection coordinators**. Some have designated all headteachers automatically; others have collected names submitted by schools. There should be such a person in every school, sixth form or FE college whatever its status.

Designated officer   A senior officer of the LEA with responsibility for child protection, usually a member of the **Area Child Protection Committee**.

Development   A child's development is defined by s.17 Children Act 1989 as including their physical, intellectual, emotional, social and behavioural development. This is intended to promote a holistic view of children and is relevant to whether the child is a **child in need**.

Direction   A requirement, written into a court order, that certain actions must be taken or not taken.

Directions appointment   A preliminary court hearing intended to reduce delay in applications for orders, fix timetables, sort out any disputes, etc.

Disclosure   A child telling an adult that they have been abused; often used in relation to sexual abuse in particular.

Duty to investigate   The statutory responsibility on the **local authority** under s.47 Children Act 1989 to make inquiries where they have reasonable cause to suspect that a child who lives in or is found in their area is suffering, or is likely to suffer **significant harm**. This is the function being requested when, for example, a headteacher asks the **social services department** to follow up a referral of a particular child. There is a companion duty on the LEA, among others, to cooperate in such investigation. (This is taken to include schools and other educational establishments.)

Ecomap   a diagram used to show a child's relationships to people outside their family, for example, school, friends, significant adults, social groups, etc.

Emergency Duty Team (EDT)   A team of social workers from the **social services department** who deal with emergencies, including child protection and mental health, outside office hours.

Emergency Protection Order (EPO)   An order under s.44 Children Act 1989 which authorizes the applicant (usually the **local authority** or the **NSPCC**), to take immediate steps to protect a child, including removing them from home if required. The applicant acquires **parental responsibility** for the duration of the order: eight days initially with a maximum extension of seven further days.

Encopresis The passing of faeces in inappropriate places; may have a dietary or emotional explanation.

Enuresis Bed-wetting, usually by children over the age of 5 or 6 or to an extent where such an event may indicate other problems, either physical or emotional.

Ex-parte A court hearing without some of the **parties** present, usually in an emergency.

Failure to thrive Used to describe children who score below an accepted level for their age on the **centile charts** system; may be an indication of inadequate food and/or care.

Family centre A place where whole families can go for help, counselling, therapy etc. Some professionals and agencies still use the term to denote residential establishments for children and they may include some provision for **accommodation** or children on a **care order**.

Family proceedings Court proceedings defined by s.8(3) Children Act 1989 which cover almost all decisions relating to the welfare of children other than child protection.

Family Proceedings Court (FPC) The new court at the level of the Magistrates Court which hears most public law applications under the Children Act 1989. Confusingly, they also deal with child protection, even though such procedures are not, strictly speaking, **family proceedings**!

Female infibulation Female genital mutilation/circumcision. An offence under a 1985 Act except on physical/mental health grounds. This is a feature of some ethnic minority cultures and seeing it as child abuse may sometimes be controversial.

Foster carer The preferred term for foster parent (as children are increasingly aware of their actual **parents** in addition to any subsequent carers and to avoid confusion between the two). Foster carers do not normally have **parental responsibility** for the children they **look after**.

Genogram A diagrammatic way of showing a child's relationships, rather like a family tree, used by social workers as a way of helping children to talk about their family life and its history. It enables important relationships to be highlighted and is a way of exploring feelings as well as facts.

Gillick competent An expression arising from the case of Gillick v. West Norfolk and Wisbech Health Authority (1985), which established that children of 'sufficient age and understanding', even if still below the age of 16, could give or refuse consent to medical treatment in their own right, without the need for parental approval. It usually relates to issues of contraception and has been challenged subsequently in cases of extreme life and death. It is reflected in a child's right to refuse medical examination, even if the subject of a **child assessment order**.

Grievous bodily harm   Major injury or trauma, with or without a weapon, including such injuries as broken bones, internal bleeding, burns, etc. More serious than **actual bodily harm**.

Grooming   The preparation of children for sexual **abuse** by establishing a relationship with the child or using normal physical contact with an ulterior motive.

Gross indecency   Difficult to define but usually involves mutual masturbation or oral sex. Only an offence if one of the participants is under 18. There is a specific offence of gross indecency with children under 14.

Guardian   A person who has taken over **parental responsibility** for a child on the death of both **parents**, either by agreement in advance or through court order (s.5 Children Act 1989). Guardian is not another word for 'carer'; that is simply a person looking after a child who is not their actual **parent**.

Guardian *ad litem* **(GAL)**   A person appointed to investigate a child's circumstances and report to the court. The GAL can appoint a solicitor for the child, is independent of the applicant/agency bringing the proceedings and is generally seen as acting on the child's behalf and ensuring that their interests are paramount.

Guidance   A **local authority** or school must act in accordance with guidance issued by the relevant Secretary of State (ie, Health or Education). Most guides to good practice in child protection operate at this level, though some are more advisory.

Harm   Includes physical and mental harm to a child's **health** and **development**.

Health   A child's health is defined by s.17 Children Act as including their physical and mental health. It is intended to cover a wide definition and is relevant to deciding whether the child is a **child in need**.

Indecent assault   Any action which is 'an affront to modesty'. There must be an **assault**, not merely indecency. This means that an invitation for a child to touch an adult's penis would not be sufficient unless there is also hostility and threat; however, actual and deliberate exposure is an offence.

Injunction   An order under the Domestic Violence and Matrimonial Proceedings Act 1976, made at a County Court, which restricts the rights of an individual in some way, usually relating to contact with partners and/or their children and made in an emergency. A more measured alternative might be a **Section 8 order** of some kind.

Investigative interview   The term often used for the interview conducted with a child in response to a referral, possibly recorded on video as provided for by the **Criminal Justice Act 1988**. Ideally, there should only be one such interview and they are conducted under **PACE** procedures.

Key worker   The social worker from the **social services department** with lead responsibility for carrying out the **child protection plan**. They should inform and liaise with key professionals from other agencies who are also involved with the child.

Life story (book)   A way of helping a child to make a record of their life, using photographs, pictures, stories, letters, etc. Can be especially valuable for children who have experienced a lot of changes.

Local authority   There is some confusion about this in the Children Act 1989. In general, it means the same as the **social services department**. But, at times, the phrase refers to the whole county/metropolitan council/London borough, that is all departments, including education. There is a sense in which the whole authority is involved in child protection and not only the social work service.

Looked after   The correct phrase to describe both children on a **care order** and those in **accommodation**, though it is sometimes used as an incorrect replacement only for those 'in care'.

Memorandum of Good Practice (1992)   A Home Office guide to the use of video recording as a way of collecting evidence from children. It does not have the force of law but is closely followed in **investigative interviews**.

Monitoring   The systematic review of plans made for a child at a **Child Case Conference**. Its function is to ensure the continued meeting of the child's needs, especially in the light of any change in circumstances.

Multiple abuse   **Abuse** of a number of children, often in the context of a group activity or organization such as a swimming club or youth group.

Munchausen's Syndrome by Proxy   Behaviour by **parents** (which some see as a mental illness), which leads them to harm their children deliberately in order to gain attention, especially from medical professionals.

National Society for the Prevention of Cruelty to Children (NSPCC) The only agency outside the **local authority** designated to bring proceedings and applications in child protection matters. Many areas operate joint investigation procedures or have close working relationships.

No order principle A fundamental requirement of all proceedings under the Children Act 1989 that making any court order must be better for the child than making no order at all.

Notice of hearing The requirement to inform all those with a right to know of any court hearing relating to a child for which they are responsible or with whom they are living. Such people then have a right to apply to become a **party** if they are not one already.

Organised abuse Sexual abuse which involves a number of perpetrators, a number of abused children and which has required an element of deliberate planning. This may include paedophile or pornographic rings and/or an element of 'ritual'. There is some dispute over the extent to which such abuse exists.

Paramountcy principle The principle inherent in the Children Act 1989 that the child's welfare is the 'paramount consideration' in any court proceedings relating to the child.

Parent Includes those with **parental responsibility** and any other adult with whom the child is living. Though the term is sometimes used to refer only to 'birth' parents, in law it has a much more general meaning. The key issue arising from the Children Act is that not all 'parents' carry the same degree of legal responsibility and authority.

Parental responsibility 'All the rights, duties, powers, responsibilities and authority which by law a **parent** has in relation to the child and his property' (s.3(1) Children Act 1989). Parental responsibility is held equally by married parents (even if they subsequently divorce): unmarried mothers hold it automatically; unmarried fathers can obtain it either by formal agreement with the mother or through the courts. It is also held by anyone with a **residence order** or an **emergency protection order** and the **local authority** share it with the parents if there is a **care order**. Knowing who has parental responsibility is fundamental to ensuring appropriate consultation with all necessary **parents**, even if they do not live with the child at present.

Party A person (or agency) with an automatic right to attend court hearings relating to children and have their views represented. Those who do not have party status automatically may be able to obtain 'leave' from the court to be joined as a party. There are no proceedings which give school staff this right without leave though views should be sought by means of reports, etc where relevant.

Permanency planning The term used by social workers when discussing long-term plans for children. This may involve rehabilitation with their **parents**, alternative parenting with either relatives or **foster carers**, **adoption**, or, occasionally, residential care.

Police and Criminal Evidence Act 1984 (PACE) Usually referred to as PACE and includes a wide range of provisions relating to the investigation of possible criminal offences, cautioning, interviewing, etc. Also gives powers to a constable to enter premises by force in an emergency.

Police protection Powers under s.46 Children Act 1989 for the police to detain a child or prevent their removal in order to protect them. The **local authority** must be contacted within 72 hours and various other persons, for example, **parents**, notified of their actions.

Police surgeon A doctor specifically trained in the collection of forensic evidence who would normally be asked to examine a child as part of the criminal investigation process following an allegation of **abuse**. (A hospital paediatrician may also be used, ideally making a joint examination at the same time in order to avoid unnecessary stress to the child.)

Post-traumatic stress disorder (PTSD) Persistent re-experience of past trauma which causes intense distress or inability to function normally. This is becoming much more widely identified as a feature in adults who were abused as children and in professionals working in the field of child protection.

Private law Family law which does not involve the state, especially matrimonial disputes and divorce. **Section 8 orders** are used primarily in this context.

Prohibited steps order An order under s.8/12 Children Act 1989 which prohibits the exercise of **parental responsibility** in some way.

Professional abuse Abuse within the care system or by others *in loco parentis* (including teachers) for which special **ACPC** procedures will apply.

Public law Law which regulates the intervention of the state into family life, especially child protection and **care** proceedings.

Reconstituted family The term often used to describe a family made up of adults and children who are not all related to each other by birth, especially step-families.

Recovery order An order under s.50 Children Act 1989 which requires any person in a position to do so, to return a child to an **authorized person**. They are made in relation to children removed from **care**, who run away or who go missing.

Representation procedures Sometimes called complaints procedures, required by s.26(3) Children Act 1989 as a means by which questions can be raised about the discharge of the functions of any **local authority**.

Residence order An order under s.8/12 Children Act 1989 which defines the person with whom a child must live. Any such person who does not already have **parental responsibility** acquires it for the duration of the order.

Risk assessment/analysis A formalized process for determining whether or not a particular child is at risk of **significant harm**. There are various models in use which measure both current and likely future risk, a key issue in determining whether a child needs to be on the **child protection register**.

Schedule 1 offender A person convicted of an offence against a child under Schedule 1 Children and Young Persons Act 1933. This includes murder, manslaughter, infanticide, incest, **assault**, sexual assault, neglect and cruelty.

Section 8 orders Four orders under the Children Act 1989: **residence order** (the replacement for 'custody'); **contact order** (the replacement for 'access'); **prohibited steps order** and **specific issue order**. These orders resolve issues concerning the exercise of **parental responsibility** towards a child and normally end at age 16.

Sibling abuse The inflicting of **harm** on a brother or sister. Some children including those with disabilities and step-children are thought to be at particular risk, though documented behaviour amounting to **abuse** is rare.

Significant harm Whether **harm** is significant turns on how the child's **health** and **development** compares with that which could reasonably be expected of a 'similar child'. This is intended to convey a sense of realism and to avoid comparison only with 'perfect' situations which could not realistically be compared with this particular child's circumstances.

Special review cases Procedures which operate to review what happened following the death or serious injury of a child within their family or a case which may arouse major public concern. (May also be known as Part 8 Reviews.)

Specific issue order An order under s.8/12 Children Act 1989 which resolves a particular dispute about the exercise of **parental responsibility** towards a child.

Social Services Department (SSD) The social work service of the **local authority** with the lead responsibility for child protection. Most departments are now separated into different sections for children's and adult's services. They are increasingly adopting a role of 'purchaser' of services from elsewhere, including the voluntary sector, rather than being a sole 'provider', especially of residential care.

Sudden infant death syndrome (SIDS)   The unexplained death of infants, usually less than 6-months old, sometimes referred to as 'cot death'.

Supervision order   An order under s.31 Children Act 1989 which places a child under the supervision of the **social services department**. (Not to be confused with an education supervision order under s.36 which is applied for, and made to, the LEA.)

Threshold criteria   The criteria for deciding whether sufficient grounds have been established to be able to prove in court that a child is suffering, or is at risk of, **significant harm**. A court must also be satisfied that the **no order principle** has been met.

Unlawful sexual intercourse (USI)   Intercourse with a child or young person under 16. The slightest degree of penetration of either the anus or the vagina constitutes an offence. Willing consent by a **Gillick competent** teenager will probably make prosecution inappropriate (especially in heterosexual sex); however, issues of power, the difference in ages, the nature of the relationship and the extent to which the consent was truly 'informed' may all be relevant.

Video suites   Centres in which children's statements are recorded on video for possible use as evidence in future criminal proceedings. They are intended to be as 'child-friendly' as possible and their location is usually confidential.

Ward of court   A child who is subject to wardship proceedings, that is, under the protection of the High Court and about whom no decisions can be made without the Court's consent.

'Working Together'   The interagency guide to child protection services issued by the Department of Health, the Home Office, the Welsh Office and the (then) Department of Education and Science in 1991.

Written agreement   An agreed basis for the provision of services between a family and a **local authority**. There should always be such an agreement when a child goes into **accommodation** which includes, for example, who is responsible for the child's education while they are living away from home.

REFERENCE

Thomas, M and Pierson, J (eds) (1995) *Dictionary of Social Work*, Collins Educational, London

Index

This index does not include references within the glossary.